Achieving Gender Equity

Strategies for the Classroom

DIANNE D. HORGAN
The University of Memphis

ALLYN and BACON
BOSTON   LONDON   TORONTO   SYDNEY   TOKYO   SINGAPORE

Editor-in-Chief, Education: Nancy Forsyth
Production Administrator: Susan McIntyre
Editorial Assistant: Christine Nelson
Cover Administrator: Suzanne Harbison
Composition Buyer: Linda Cox
Manufacturing Buyer: Megan Cochran
Editorial-Production Service: Ruttle, Shaw & Wetherill, Inc.

Copyright © 1995 by Allyn and Bacon
A Division of Paramount Publishing
160 Gould Street
Needham Heights, Massachusetts 02194

Library of Congress Cataloging-in-Publication Data

Horgan, Dianne D.
    Achieving gender equity : strategies for the classroom / Dianne D. Horgan.
      p.   cm.
    Includes bibliographic references and index.
    ISBN 0–205–15459–X
    1. Sex discrimination in education—United States. 2. Sexism in
education—United States. 3. Sex differences in education—United
States. 4. Educational equalization—United States. I. Title.
LC212.82.H67 1995
370.19'345—dc20   94–328
                                                                  CIP

Printed in the United States of America
10 9 8 7 6 5 4 3 2 1   99 98 97 96 95 94

To my androgynous children, Kelly and Alec,
who have taught me more about child and adolescent development
than I could have ever learned from the scientific literature.

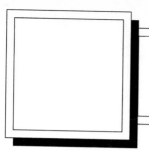

Contents

Part II: Toward a Solution

Preface

Typically, girls earn better grades than boys and present far fewer disciplinary problems. Yet they are more likely to suffer from low self-esteem and low self-confidence. They are less likely to select challenging courses, particularly in math and science. When faced with a difficult problem, girls are less likely than boys to persist. Girls are more likely to avoid tasks in which there is a likelihood of failure. When they are adults, young women then enter the workplace with serious internal barriers to success. They don't believe in themselves, and they haven't subjected themselves to the most challenging learning situations.

Many boys, especially minority boys and boys of lower socioeconomic status, are also at risk. Teachers often assume that boys will misbehave and dislike school. Often, they are treated more harshly than girls. Boys are more likely to fail, drop out, misbehave, and exhibit poor motivation. Minority boys may feel serious peer pressure to resist Anglo-American, middle-class school values. The situation for minority boys and for all girls is similar in that—with all good intentions—teachers expect less from them, interact less with them, and send them "low-ability" messages.

This book focuses on how teachers can help both girls and boys develop the self-confidence and skills necessary to be successful. In today's classrooms, girls are rarely told they can't do math or science. Textbooks show pictures of women and men in both career and nurturing roles. In preschools, little boys play in the housekeeping center, and little girls play with trucks and blocks. Yet, although doors are opening, the data continue to show that young women have lower self-esteem, lower career aspirations, and lower rates of participation in math and science. Why? Part of the reason is that many women still face *internal* barriers to success. These are attitudes and fears that result from subtle differences in the ways in which girls and boys are socialized. These more subtle parts of the socialization process are the focus of this book. Even people who are trying to encourage girls may send them negative messages. For example, well-intentioned math teachers may fear discouraging girls, so offer them less criticism than boys, thereby teaching them less. Or they may offer girls premature help, inadvertently suggesting to girls that they probably won't be able to solve the problem alone.

Recent writings in various fields of psychology (cognitive, social cognitive, attribution theory, motivation theory) have produced a great deal of research relevant to this topic, yet relatively little *practical* literature has been written from this perspective. In this book, I have tried to address practical applications.

Achieving Gender Equity has four chapters: Chapters 1 and 2 describe subtle differences in socialization and how they result in both barriers to girls' success and problems for boys. Chapter 3 presents thirteen strategies for how teachers can modify their classrooms and their personal behavior to counteract some of the negative motivational messages that young girls receive and to create an enhanced learning environment that will benefit all students. Chapter 4 offers suggestions on how to deal with parents and engage them in achieving gender equity for their children.

Chapters 1 and 2 include case studies and many examples. Chapters 3 and 4 focus on how to make positive changes in the classroom. Included are a "gender-bias audit," a series of checklists, strategies, and suggestions. The suggested strategies will not only help achieve gender equity, they will also help create a better overall learning environment for *all* children.

ACKNOWLEDGMENTS

I'm grateful to my family, students, and colleagues who read and critiqued earlier drafts of this book. I'm also indebted to Carol Wade and Patricia B. Campbell, who provided many excellent suggestions. Nancy Forsyth's enthusiasm and ideas helped shape the book, and I'm very grateful for her expertise. Special acknowledgment goes to my son Alec, who served as chief research assistant and amateur editor. Thanks, too, to our dog Woody, who sat with me through every word I wrote, licking my feet for encouragement. Gratitude, too, goes to my husband Terry, who helped at every step in the process of putting this book together.

1 Girls in the Classroom and Beyond

It doesn't seem possible, she thought, that I've been teaching at East High for ten years now. Looking through the old year book, Emily Butler smiled, remembering the young people who'd been her first students. That class would always be special to her because it was her first year of teaching. She hadn't been much older than her seniors. She was really looking forward to tonight's reunion.

I wonder if they will remember me as clearly as I remember them, she mused. It will be fun to see how they've turned out. There was so much talent in that group. It's exciting to think that I helped shape them into responsible, mature adults. There's Monica's picture—such a lovely young woman. I'll never forget Monica. She never made anything but an A. She wouldn't even consider taking Physics because it might spoil her perfect GPA! She worked so hard and was so eager to please. What a perfect student she was. Oh, and there's Paul. Paul, who couldn't sit still. He was so bright, but wouldn't turn in his homework. I remember him sitting in the back of the room, talking and passing notes. I used to call on him to try to make him pay attention. Monica and Paul were both in my third-period class—what a group that was. Jessica and Nicole were in there, too. What great girls. I could always count on them. They always read their assignments and raised their hands. I can remember them waving their hands at me. I'd smile and look around for someone to call on, someone who didn't look very alert. Usually Paul. The girls told me I paid more attention to the boys, but I'd laugh and explain that I had to. Boys are just harder to teach. The girls used to complain that we always read books about men, written by men. How in the world would I ever have managed to get boys like Paul to read "women's" books? When I assigned a poem by Emily Dickinson, the boys nearly gagged.

I remember how hard I tried to encourage my girls. Girls have such great opportunities now. I always told them that they could be anything they wanted to be. I tried hard to give them lots of extra praise to build their self-confidence. I'll never forget Monica's term paper. It really wasn't as good as she could do, but I knew how upset she'd be if she didn't get glowing comments. She would have been crushed if I'd handed it back all covered in red ink. Then I think of all the time I spent marking Paul's paper. I don't think he ever bothered to proofread anything. I went over his papers with a fine-toothed comb. I sure hope he learned grammar from my class. I went kind of easy on the girls because I didn't want to discourage them. Monica and Jessica weren't sure about college at the beginning of the year, but I encouraged them. I wanted them to know they could get A's. How excited Monica and Jessica were when they got scholarships to college. Jessica told me how lucky she was and Monica insisted she didn't deserve it. They hung around me, always asking my advice and seeking reassurance. They made me feel needed. I can't wait to see what they're doing now.

That night, Emily Butler watched the mature adults enter the gym. It sure wasn't like ten years ago when they came spilling into pep rallies. She loved the daily interactions with her students, but there was something really exciting about seeing her students as adults. Now she was going to find out if she'd prepared them for the real world.

Almost immediately, Monica came rushing up to her.

"Mrs. Butler! You haven't changed a bit! I'm so glad to see you!"

Monica looked great and Emily was thrilled to be remembered.

"Monica, I'm so glad to see you, too. Tell me what you've been doing."

Monica had finished college and was now working as a receptionist. Emily was a little disappointed. Somehow she thought Monica would be in a professional position, but Monica seemed happy and said she enjoyed meeting people. The job wasn't demanding, but it suited her.

"And," she continued, "you'll never guess who my boss is!"

To Emily's surprise, it was Paul. Paul who could never get his homework in on time was now running a major business.

"Paul and I went to the same college, you know. It took him an extra year to graduate. You know how Paul likes to party. But when he graduated, he started with the firm and within three years was the branch manager."

"Monica," Emily asked, "Do you want more from a career? Do you have plans to move up?" Monica sighed. "Well I'd thought about getting an MBA. That would help me a lot, but you know an MBA requires all that accounting. It's really a very quantitative degree. You remember how bad I am in math. I just don't think I could do it."

Then Jessica and Nicole arrived, hugging and kissing both Monica and Emily. Well, thought Emily, I bet these two have been more successful.

But Jessica and Nicole, like Monica, had not achieved what Emily would have thought. They were among the brightest, most motivated students she'd had. Nicole had started in the management training program of a large company right after college, along with several other East High graduates. Emily was struck by a sudden insight: the men were now moving up to middle-management positions. Most of the women were behind them. What a reversal from high school. In her class, it was the girls who did everything thoroughly and on time.

This reunion was not turning out to be much fun. As Emily talked with more and more of her old students, the pattern was unmistakable. The men were more successful in their careers than the women. Sure, some of the women had chosen not to have careers and some had put their careers on hold to be full-time mothers, but even those young women without children were behind the men. A few young women were very successful, but they were the minority. But by and large, things didn't look equal. Emily wondered what had happened.

Emily Butler kept brooding about her experience at the reunion. Could it be that she and the other teachers at East High had not prepared the girls for the real world? Emily had seen television reports about gender equity, but she knew they didn't apply to her. Other teachers might favor boys, but not Emily. She liked her female students. She wanted them to excel.

Monday at school, she raised her concerns with some other teachers. They agreed that there was a problem, but didn't see how they could be part of it.

"It's the parents," suggested Mr. Mullins. "They just don't expect much of daughters."

"It's sex discrimination," offered Ms. Wang. "Men just won't promote women. Here at East High, we treat everyone the same and prepare them well, but discrimination in the workplace is the problem."

The other teachers agreed, but Emily insisted that maybe there was something that they as teachers could do to enhance young women's opportunities. She talked with the principal, who suggested an in-service program. The principal was aware of the problem and was under some pressure because of Title IX of the Higher Education Amendments of 1972, which prohibits sex discrimination in schools. As a response to Title IX, the school had made sure all courses were open to both girls and boys, and the girls' sports program had been expanded.

Back in the teachers' lounge, several people groaned, "Oh, no. What a drag, another in-service. We're progressive and aware. We don't need anyone telling us to encourage girls. We already do that. Just look around school and see how well girls do. More girls than boys make honor roll. Look at how many of our girls go on to college. There may be a problem, but it's not with us."

The "problem" at East High is very real and it's everywhere. Girls do well through school, but fall behind after they leave school. In 1972, the U.S. Department of Education began the National Longitudinal Study (NLS) a national study of over 22,000 high school students.[1] These students have been followed up over twenty years and offer a clear picture of how American women are doing. The good news is that more and more American women are becoming better and better educated. The bad news is that women's rewards in the workplace don't match their academic achievements. Starting in 1972 when these students graduated from high school, women ranked higher in their class than did men. Even though women made better grades in high school, men scored higher on both the SAT and the ACT. The differences are not just in math: Men have even outscored women on the *verbal* part of the SAT since 1972. In 1992, more than 60 percent of National Merit Semifinalists (based exclusively on PSAT scores) were male.[2] On the PSAT, verbal scores are doubled to minimize sex differences; without this effort, even a higher percentage of semifinalists would be male. Despite more attention to gender equity, today's girls are still not scoring as well as boys, particularly in math. Reasons for this are complex and controversial, but differences in course work taken is one clear contributing factor.[3] Males tend to take more rigorous courses. In the NLS sample, 35.3 percent of men and only 18.2 percent of women took a college-prep curriculum of more than four semesters in both math and science. When we look at SAT or ACT scores, the 18.2 percent of women who took these rigorous courses scored a little higher than the men. This means that when women take the same courses, they score as well as (or better than) men. But because so few women take these rigorous courses and therefore are not prepared to compete, the differences at the high end of the SAT scores greatly favor men: Even now, 89 percent of those students who score above 750 on the math part of the SAT are male![4]

The NLS study found that men had higher educational aspirations, yet women actually achieved more in college. Women earned their degrees in less time and made better grades. But men and women took very different courses in college: Men took more math, computer science, statistics, engineering, and business courses. Women took more courses in languages, education, and the performing arts. The women who chose traditionally male fields, however, had higher GPAs. For example, in science and math, female majors had an average GPA of 3.18, while the average for men was 2.98.

Because so few women chose to take math and science, you might think that they were the brightest women. If that were the case—that female math and science majors are the cream of the crop, while male math and science majors are more "ordinary Joes"—then you'd expect female mathematicians and scientists to experience greater, or at least equal, job success. The NLS study included salary data for the 1972 graduates at age 32 (in 1986): men who majored in physical sciences and math earned an average of $32,209 per year. Thirty-two-year-old women, with the same major and *without* children, earned only $22,777! Women with children earned only $17,915. These differentials aren't the result of differences in years worked; the men averaged 5.84 years; the women without children, 5.51; and the women with children, 5.13. Obviously, the men got better-paying jobs and progressed faster, while the women accepted lower-paying jobs. What these data show is that women's skills are undervalued. The same math and science knowledge and skills have less worth in the marketplace when held by women.

In 1992, *Science* reported on the status of women in math and science.[5] The news is not good. Despite the fact that more and more undergraduate women are majoring in math and science, they are not moving through the "achievement pipeline" at the rate that men are. For example, there is only *one* female mathematician in the National Academy of Sciences. At the top ten math departments in the nation, there are three hundred tenured men and only *two* tenured women. Throughout the country, women are 40 percent of the lecturers and instructors in math and science, 29 percent of assistant professors, 19 percent of associate professors, and only 8 percent of full professors. Neena Schwartz, a member of the first National Academy of Sciences committee on women, reported that back in 1974 she thought ". . . all you had to do was get more women into the pool—into graduate schools and tenure-track positions—and automatically they would move onto the faculty and into industry and so on. Well, we were naive."[6]

The authors in the *Science* series of articles blame a number of factors. One is treatment by teachers: a study by the American Association for the Advancement of Science (AAAS) found that women in college science classes were treated more negatively than men by both the faculty and other students. Lack of self-confidence is another factor. This not only affects students, but even female faculty. Sue Geller surveyed editors of math journals and was told that female mathematicians often submit their best work to less prestigious journals than would be appropriate.[7] A third factor is lack of mentors and role models. The difficulty of combining a family with a career, as well as a lack of "family friendly" university and company policies, also contributes to the problem. This is no doubt why, according to a 1990 survey of the American Chemical Society, 38 percent of female chemists are single, compared to only 18 percent of men in the field. Finally, the authors report that sexism is still strong, particularly in math. Lynne Butler, an assistant professor of math at Princeton, left Princeton because of blatant sexist remarks, such as a colleague who said, "I feel bad about it, but I really do feel women are genetically inferior in math."[8] Sadly, the problem for women in math and science is worse in the United States than in many other countries. Here, only 3 percent of faculty members in physics are women: Japan—not known for feminism—has 6 percent; Belgium, 11 percent; France and Italy, 23 percent; and the former USSR, 30 percent.

According to the NLS, even in female-dominated fields, men earned more. Men who majored in education were earning an average of $21,651 at age thirty-two, compared to $18,544 for women without children. These differences in the workplace aren't because women are less motivated—their higher grades and faster graduation rate in college clearly reflect a strong motivation to succeed.

Doubtlessly, some of the difference results from discrimination. Discrimination affects women in three ways. First is direct discrimination against individual women: women are simply not treated as well as men. An employer might, for example, refuse to promote a worker simply because she is female or may hire a less qualified man over a better qualified women. Second is discrimination against female-dominated *careers*. Jobs that have traditionally been held by women pay less than jobs traditionally held by men. But the third type of discrimination is more subtle. Stereotypes of women lead people (yes, women as well as men) to place women in different kinds of roles than men, to expect less from them, to judge them by different standards, and to interpret their performance differently.

The first and second kinds of direct discrimination are decreasing as more and more women enter a broader range of careers; but the third shows little signs of letting up. The third type results from sex-role stereotyping. Stereotyping affects not only those who hire women, but women's own development. Women suffer from a lack of self-confidence and learn to devalue their own performance, expect less, and avoid risks. The result is that women must face not only external barriers to success (some of which are subtle), but they also have to overcome their internal barriers.

New research suggests that these internal barriers are rooted in the socialization process—which includes school experiences. In 1992, the American Association of University Women (AAUW) issued a shocking report, entitled *How Schools Shortchange Girls*.[9] It documented that girls are not receiving the same quality or even quantity of education as boys. Based on a thorough review of recent work,[10] they found a consistent pattern of inequity at all grade levels, even through college. Teachers interact with boys more, ask them more challenging questions, give them more precise feedback, and listen to them more. To make matters worse, few teachers were aware of these differences in their behavior. Most denied that they treated girls and boys differently and were shocked when researchers showed them videotaped evidence. These differences are widespread; virtually all teachers treat boys and girls differently in the classroom, at least some of the time. Besides subtle messages sent by teachers that girls' opinions and interests count for less than those of boys, boys freely harass and embarrass girls with little interference from teachers or parents. These experiences result in a "chilly" emotional climate for girls.[11]

Research in most areas of the social sciences often is conflicting; some studies will support one perspective, while others find contradictory results. The studies on gender equity, however, paint a consistent picture: study after study, by different teams of researchers, in different classrooms, in different parts of the country, in different subjects, with different teachers, and with different age groups show gender inequity.[12] These studies are carefully controlled; the results are carefully documented. Typically, they involve videotaping many hours of classroom interactions and then several independent observers score the tapes, using carefully designed and objective scoring forms.

Not only do boys receive more of the teacher's attention, but it is often the case that a few highly competent (usually Anglo-American) boys, receive the lion's share of the attention. The attention that minority students receive may differ also. One study reports that African-American boys tend to have fewer interactions with the teacher than either Anglo-American girls or boys, and that they are much more likely to receive qualified praise: "That's good, but . . . ." Other studies suggest that teachers explain good performance differently, based on ethnic background as well as gender. Anglo-American boys, who do well are assumed to be "smart," while high-achieving minority students and Anglo-American girls are more likely to have their success explained by unusual effort.[13]

Our fictional high school teacher, "Emily Butler," is a dedicated professional, whose heart is in the right place. By now, you've probably figured out that her scenario reflects some gender inequity. She is not unusual. Not only have I known many Emily Butlers in the almost twenty years that I've taught educational psychology, but I've made many of the same mistakes myself. As a mother of both a boy and a girl, despite great effort to treat them equally, I frequently find my behavior is inconsistent with my theories of equality. All teachers (and students hoping to become teachers), no matter how liberated and how well intentioned, have been socialized so that we have different expectations of and different ways of behaving toward girls and boys. Gender equity is not just something for "those old-fashioned teachers" to worry about; we all need to work hard to provide girls and boys with the same educational opportunities.

The AAUW study points to two other general areas in which girls are short-changed: the formal curriculum and what they call the "evaded" curriculum. The formal curriculum presents books and materials that contain many more references and pictures of men and boys. When women and girls are included, they often are stereotyped. In recent years, textbooks have come under increasing scrutiny and now show a more balanced view. In children's literature, however, many books present negative images of women and girls. Older books (the ones that you remember from your childhood) are more likely to show gender bias. Researchers looked at sex roles in books that had won the Caldecott Medal from 1953 to 1971. The ratio of male to female characters was 11 to 1. The ratio of male animal to female animal characters was 95 to 1![14] More recent work still shows a discrepancy, but not nearly so great. A study of Caldecott books from the 1980s found 57 percent of the characters were male. Other studies of children's literature find that although included more often, girls and women are frequently in supporting roles and shown in stereotypical ways. Boys are more likely to be depicted as self-sufficient and capable, while girls are more likely to be shown as helpless.

The AAUW report also describes the "evaded curriculum"—what's *not* taught. Students are not taught about women's contributions or very much about topics of special interest to girls and women. In all courses, the use of works by and about women needs to be expanded. The authors conclude that the school curriculum needs to include more material focusing specifically on women and issues of special interest to girls.

The results of this "miseducation" of girls can be seen in a number of ways. The most obvious is the difference between the sexes in later achievements. But studies also indicate some earlier problems with self-esteem. Carol Gilligan and colleagues report that as middle-class girls reach adolescence, they experience a serious drop in self-esteem.[15] They note: ". . . Girls at this time have been observed to lose their vitality, their resilience, their immunity to depression, their sense of themselves and their character."[16] Gilligan believes culture and the socialization process, including schools, are largely to blame. Low self-esteem and low self-confidence prevent young women from choosing challenging schoolwork, which then limits their career choices. Myra and David Sadker and colleagues have been leaders in research on girls in school and report that among Anglo-American high school girls, 61 percent report very low self-confidence and low personal satisfaction.[17] This is about twice the rate among boys. Most studies of Anglo-American, middle-class girls show a decline in self-esteem and self-confidence as girls enter adolescence. The AAUW study, for example, found that while 60 percent of elementary girls were "happy the way I am," only 29 percent of high school girls felt the same way.[18] Among boys, the percentage dropped from 69 percent in elementary school to 46 percent in high school.

This drop in self-esteem appears to be mostly a middle-class, Anglo-American phenomenon. Among elementary school girls in the AAUW study, African-American and Hispanic-American girls were more likely to be "happy the way I am" than were Anglo-American girls (65 percent and 68 percent versus 55 percent for Anglo-American girls). By high school, Anglo-American and Hispanic-American girls dropped to 22 percent and 30 percent, while 58 percent of African-American girls still were "happy the way I am."

By most measures such as grades, Anglo-American, middle-class girls do exceedingly well in our schools. These girls with such low esteem have been raised in an era in which women are encouraged to "be all they can be." Why don't they feel good about themselves? These girls may be most influenced by society's messages that girls and women are valued for their appearance and passivity rather than for their abilities. Further, Anglo-American middle-class girls receive mixed messages. On the one hand, they are told they can do anything boys can, but they are then bombarded with stereotypical images of women as sex objects who are helpless and weak. They are expected to succeed, but are told they don't have "the right stuff." Since minority girls and women are less frequently seen in the media and less frequently told they can be anything they aspire to be, the messages they receive are not so mixed. Minority girls are under less pressure to "have it all." Carol Dweck reports some equally disturbing data about *gifted* young women.[19] Gifted girls are the most capable young women, the ones experiencing the most success. Yet they, too, doubt their abilities, despite the fact that they've had much evidence to the contrary. These are the bright girls who've made A's in all their math courses, but don't sign up for advanced math courses because of self-doubt. Their successes don't ensure their self-confidence or high self-esteem.[20] The problem for girls and women, however, cuts deeper than a lack of self-confidence or low expectations. Because girls are more likely to avoid challenging tasks and risks, they may actually *learn* less. Combined with the fact that teachers give girls less effective feedback, which also contributes to less learning, this means that many girls leave school seriously handicapped against professional success.

What can teachers do about gender inequity? The new research on gender inequity falls into two main categories: (1) negative messages that teachers inadvertently send girls, and (2) the often dysfunctional ways that girls explain their successes and failures. Psychologists call the process by which people explain or interpret their success or failure, *attribution*. Each of these areas of research offers ideas for enhancing girls' educational opportunities.

NEGATIVE MESSAGES

Even people who try to encourage girls may send negative messages. For example, well intentioned math teachers may fear discouraging girls and consequently offer them less criticism than boys. Or they may offer girls premature help, suggesting to girls that they probably won't be able to solve the problem alone and that it's not even worth the struggling to try. If a teacher has confidence in a student, the teacher is more likely to let the student struggle a little longer. Or, teachers may ask boys the hard questions and ask girls the easier ones, which suggests to students that only boys are capable of answering harder questions. Similarly, when asking a question of a bright student, teachers wait or probe for a good answer. When teachers ask boys questions, they do just that: they wait longer and they keep probing until they get the right answer. But, with girls, they are not as persistent, which suggests to students that girls are not expected to get the answer. When boys get the wrong answer, teachers are more likely to give corrective feedback and admonish them to work harder. When girls get the wrong answer, teachers are more likely to praise them for their efforts and simply tell them the correct answer.[21] This tells students that, for boys, more effort will improve performance and thus encourages boys to persist toward a correct solution. But girls learn that their hard work didn't lead to successful performance and the teacher lacks confidence in their ability to solve the problem.

In classroom discussions, girls typically are better prepared and more eager to contribute. They wave their hands, but the teacher is more likely to call on one of the few boys who has raised his hand.[22] When a boy makes a comment, the teacher gives it more recognition, often working it into the discussion or return-ing to his point. Girls' comments usually receive less elaboration and have less impact on the discussion.

Another way that teachers sometimes send "low-ability" messages is by offering excessive praise. When someone says that we have done a good job, we interpret it to mean that our performance was equal to, if not better than, ex-pected. When we receive *lots* of praise, that means we did a whole lot better than expected. Imagine if you and the student next to you both got back an exam marked "93." His has nothing else written on it. Yours is packed with "smiley faces" and glowing comments. At first, you enjoy reading these, but then you look at his paper and begin to wonder why the teacher thinks you need so much more encouragement. Why is this such a big achievement for you and such an ordinary one for him? Is it because success is the norm for him and something extraordi-nary for you? The problem here, of course, is not that you received praise. It's that there was *differential* praise for *equivalent* performance. Teachers praise girls more, which means that boys are often *under*praised. Teachers need to praise students, but they must be very careful that their praise doesn't send messages of low expectation. They must be careful to give equal praise for equal work. Too much praise can be worse than too little!

It's no wonder that girls begin to doubt their abilities when they are praised for trying hard and then are not expected to continue struggling to succeed at the task. We tell a girl, "That's okay; you did your best and besides, it was really hard," while we tell a boy, "If you keep at it, you'll get it." Is it any wonder that boys learn to persist and girls learn that their best isn't good enough? Many of the negative messages that girls receive are *not* the result of negative feelings or intentions toward girls. Indeed, teachers often prefer the quieter, more conform-ing, eager-to-please girls over the rowdy boys. The problems arise when we protect girls from their mistakes, avoid criticizing them, take care not to hurt their feelings, and reward them for dependency. You'll notice this is just the pattern that Emily Butler showed in her own teaching.

Teachers rarely are aware of these patterns; most argue that it's not true in their classroom. But study after study with careful, videotaped observations shows the same pattern at all levels, even through college.

Let's look again at some of the things that Emily Butler remembered. Can you now analyze her statements for indications of gender bias? Think about what you've read so far and see how it applies. Look for evidence of differential expectations or behavior toward girls versus boys. Do you think Emily Butler sent any negative messages? See if you detect any stereotyping. Do the girls display lower self-confidence? After each of Emily Butler's statements in the Exhibit below, write your ideas about how they may reflect gender bias.

Each of these comments is discussed at the end of this Chapter (see page 21). Look back and see if you caught all of the gender equity concerns.

EXHIBIT

1. There's Monica's picture—such a lovely young woman.

   _____

   _____

2. Monica never made anything but an A. She wouldn't even consider taking Physics because it might spoil her perfect GPA!

   _____

   _____

3. She worked so hard and was so eager to please. What a perfect student she was.

   _____

   _____

4. What great girls! I could always count on them. They always read their assignments and raised their hands. I can remember them waving their hands at me. I'd smile and look around for someone to call on, someone who didn't look very alert. Usually Paul!

   _____

   _____

5. The girls told me I paid more attention to the boys, but I'd laugh and explain that I had to. Boys are just harder to teach.

   _____

   _____

6. The girls used to complain that we always read books about men, written by men. How in the world would I ever have managed to get boys like Paul to read "women's" books?

   _____

   _____

(continued)

7. I remember how hard I tried to encourage my girls. Girls have such great opportunities now. I always told them they could be anything they wanted to be.

   _____

   _____

8. I tried hard to give the girls lots of extra praise to build their self-confidence.

   _____

   _____

9. I'll never forget Monica's term paper. It really wasn't as good as she could do, but I knew how upset she'd be if she didn't get glowing comments. She would have been crushed if I'd handed it back all covered in red ink! I went kind of easy on the girls because I didn't want to discourage them. Then I think of all the time I spent marking Paul's paper! I went over his papers with a fine-toothed comb.

   _____

   _____

10. They hung around me, always asking my advice and seeking reassurance. They made me feel needed.

    _____

    _____

11. Well I'd thought about getting an MBA. That would help me a lot, but you know an MBA requires all that accounting. You remember how bad I am in math! I just don't think I could do it.

    _____

    _____

KILLING GIRLS WITH KINDNESS

The pattern we see is that girls often get "kid-glove" treatment. Teachers like girls, appreciate their cooperative, quiet behavior, and see them as more sensitive. Teachers believe girls are more likely to have tried, while boys are more likely not to have given their best efforts. Teachers push boys more and worry less about hurting their feelings. They also don't really expect quite as much from girls when it comes to math and science.

A similar pattern sometimes happens with minority students of both sexes. Teachers want to be especially nice to them, so they give them lots of extra praise and help. They feel sorry for these "victims" of society and unconsciously send them more "victim" messages: "You poor baby, you can't be expected to do well." But "victim" feedback often results in victim-like thinking. People do things to victims; victims can't help themselves.

A good example of how important it is to avoid the victim syndrome comes from one of my favorite examples of a good role model for teachers: a physical therapist. When I required physical therapy for an injured shoulder, I whined and complained that the weights were too heavy, the exercises too painful, and that I really didn't need to be able to lift my arm any higher. It wasn't my fault that my shoulder was injured; I shouldn't have to endure any more pain. I, after all, was the victim here and deserved sympathy. Did my therapist say, "Oh, you poor baby. I know it hurts. You don't have to do any more. Just go home and relax"? No! She had been well trained. I was told that I could regain the use of my arm *if* I worked hard. She would help, but I had to do it. She knew I could. It would be tough, but she was confident that I could do it. She didn't put up with my victim talk and she certainly didn't send me any victim messages! The result, of course, is that I have full use of my right arm again. All physical therapists are trained to behave this way; few teachers are.

Similarly, counselors refer to people who've experienced violent crimes or disasters as *survivors* rather than *victims* because the word survivor connotes someone who is responsible for her own survival, while victim connotes someone who has no control over her life. The person may not have been able to control what happened to her, but she can control how she will deal with it and how she'll triumph over adversity. The message is that you can't change the past, but can exert some control over the future.

THE ATTRIBUTION PUZZLE

As we've seen, girls typically make better grades than boys and present far fewer disciplinary problems, yet they are more likely to suffer from low self-esteem and low self-confidence. Despite their good grades, they are less likely to select challenging courses, particularly in math and science. When faced with a difficult problem, girls are less likely than boys to persist and more likely to become frustrated. One explanation for these puzzling facts is that girls and boys tend to have different *attributional styles*. Attributions, you'll recall, are the explanations that people give for success or failure. In study after study, researchers have found alarming differences in how boys and girls typically explain success and failure.[23]

Explanations about success and failure involve beliefs about ability, effort, and luck. These beliefs are shaped by environment. Different cultures, for example, explain success and failure differently. American mothers are more likely to believe their children's academic success is due to ability, while Asian mothers are more likely to attribute their children's success to hard work. While explanations of success and failure differ, even within the same culture, children begin to form consistent beliefs about reasons for their success and failure.

A child's level of cognitive functioning and maturity also affects these beliefs. For example, Carol Dweck explains that children's beliefs about ability change with age.[24] Young children hold the belief that ability is *incremental*. People learn more and more and get smarter and smarter. This is a charming stage of life, when children believe that because their parents and teachers are older and more experienced, they must also be smarter. By late childhood, however, children's theories of intelligence begin to change. They begin to see ability as a *trait* and as fairly stable. They believe that if someone is "smart," he or she will always be smart and if someone is "dumb," he or she will always be dumb. (Sometime soon after, children decide their parents and teachers really aren't too smart.) Dweck argues that these changes come about for several reasons. First, children become more aware of their performance relative to others and better able to judge performance. In Piaget's terms, they become less *egocentric*. They notice that they don't run the fastest, draw the best pictures, or always know the answer. What's more, they begin to notice a pattern: the same few students seem to always do the best, while the same few are typically at the bottom. They become aware of the academic pecking order and the fact that it's relatively stable.

Very young children can each believe that they're the smartest, fastest, strongest, or cutest. But as they mature, it becomes painfully obvious that not everyone can be the best. When they run a race, only one person is the fastest. What's more, in race after race, it becomes clear that the same people tend to be fast and the same ones come in last. School tasks change, too. In preschool and kindergarten, the criteria for success are pretty broad. Any number of pictures are acceptably drawn or colored. Even purple cows are okay. But in higher grades, the range of right answers becomes narrower and narrower. In math class, for example, there's just one acceptable answer, no matter how neat your paper is or how hard you tried.

In terms of attribution, seeing ability as a stable trait means that success resulting from ability is highly predictive of future success: once smart, always smart. Boys, more than girls, tend to see their successes as resulting from their own efforts and ability. Because ability is seen as stable and effort is under their own control, when boys succeed they are more likely to believe they will continue to succeed. Personal success, however, looks different to most girls. Girls tend to attribute their successes more to *external causes* such as luck or the situation. A girl who did well, for example, might believe that the test was easy or that the teacher liked her. Because these perceived causes are not under her control, she doesn't see her success as predictive of future successes.

The reasons for these differences in attribution are complex, but they seem to be based on different socialization practices. The kinds of classroom interactions that we've discussed contribute. Boys are sent the message that they can improve their performance if they try harder, while girls are sent "low-ability" messages. Boys are praised for being smart, while girls may be praised for being cute. Girls are supposed to be modest; boys are expected to brag and take credit for their accomplishments. If you think carefully about the classroom differences that we've discussed, you should see the general pattern: for boys, success is linked with effort; for girls, success is often perceived as a fluke.

Lots of success doesn't "cure" the tendency to view success as externally controlled. The most successful girls are often the ones most likely to lack self confidence, to be afraid of failure. Why do successful girls persist in downgrading their successes after repeated success? Why do these girls cling to the belief that their successes are flukes? It is precisely because they succeed so often—they receive frequent messages (often indirectly) that they were lucky to succeed or that they succeeded because others helped them. In addition, because the feedback girls receive is often not contingent on their performance, they may not learn to accurately assess their own work. This means they have to rely on the teacher or others to tell them whether their work is good or not. Girls tend to be more focused on how others react to them than are boys, so that when others tell them they were "lucky" to succeed, they pay close attention. The more they succeed, the more they come to believe (and hear) that they were lucky and it's, therefore, unlikely the luck will last. Their own experiences are consistent with what they see on television and what they read: women and girls' success is likely to be a fluke or based on appearance or personality or others' help; men and boy's success comes from their own efforts and abilities.

If success is not seen as resulting from one's own efforts or abilities, it's not much of an uplifting experience. It's difficult to take risks or simply "hang in there" for the long haul if you don't get full satisfaction from your successes. Success should insulate you against failure. This is one reason that women are more likely to suffer from emotional and intellectual burnout and are less likely to persist in the face of repeated failure. Providing the right kind of feedback is one important way to help girls receive the full psychological benefits of their successes. Teachers are usually attuned to giving feedback after failure that won't damage young egos, but few people have ever thought about the importance of giving the "right kind" of praise.

The story is equally lopsided when students fail. Boys are less likely to be bogged down by their failures, while failure for girls is more debilitating. Failure is much more damaging to self-esteem if you believe it's entirely *your* fault and results from general inadequacies. These differences in attributional style mean that many women leave school with two serious barriers to success: they don't believe in themselves and they haven't subjected themselves to the most challenging learning situations. Boys' attributional style leads to problems, too. They tend to overlook their own role in failure and hence miss opportunities to learn from mistakes.

Students learn how to interpret success and failure from the way in which their teachers and parents react to success and failure. Besides reacting to the students' performance, adults model the explanations for success and failure. The mother who "explains" her promotion as luck or the father who "explains" his termination as unfair is teaching children what "causes" success and failure. Children learn from our examples, and educators have to learn to model appropriate attributional styles.

Attributional style contributes to motivation. When teachers think of motivational problems, they tend to focus on the obvious: failure to turn in work, not trying to succeed, and the like. These problems are easy to diagnose and teachers never overlook them—because they cause problems for the teacher. These are also the sorts of motivational problems that are typical of boys. But girls often have more subtle, "hidden" motivational problems. These rarely cause any problems for the teacher. One "girl" style of motivational problem is an outgrowth of the attributional style that we've been discussing. A girl, for example, may work hard, try desperately to please the teacher, do everything just the way the teacher wants, and make good grades. So what's the problem? The problem is that the need to succeed in these ways may make a girl unwilling to tackle difficult challenges. She may shy away from hard courses. She may avoid expressing her own view and prefer to "regurgitate" the teacher's view. Later, she may choose a "safe" career rather than the one in which she has great talent. Later still, she may experience burnout. This motivational problem is just as real and just as serious as the problems more typical of boys. It's one problem, however, that teachers not only overlook, but often contribute to by rewarding girls for conformity rather than originality and for passivity rather than assertion. The typical "boy" motivational problem presents itself in the classroom. The effects of the typical "girl" problem often go unnoticed until years later. In summary, educators often overlook their female students' motivational problems because of two features: (1) typical "girl" motivational problems rarely have a negative impact on teachers, and (2) the main effects of the problem are not evident until years later.

Let's think again about "Emily Butler." Can you identify the dysfunctional attribution present below?

How excited Monica and Jessica were when they got scholarships to college. Jessica told me how lucky she was and Monica insisted she didn't deserve it.

Monica and Jessica saw their success as resulting from luck. They didn't feel they had the ability or had put in the necessary effort to deserve success. They didn't believe their success was *contingent* on their abilities or efforts. Instead, their success depended on external circumstances, such as other people or luck.

Attributional style can be changed through a process called *attribution retraining*. Teachers can teach students to interpret their successes and failures in a more productive light. This is one of the main strategies for bringing about gender equity in the classroom.

We've focused so far on girls' problems, but remember that gender inequity hurts boys, too.

PROBLEMS FOR BOYS

Schools present problems for many boys as well as for girls. More boys fail grades, drop out of school, are assigned to special education classes, and become disciplinary problems.[25] Teachers often have negative expectations about boys: boys are expected to dislike school and misbehave. Since most teachers are women, schools emphasize and reward more stereotypical feminine behavior. Boys often feel like outsiders in a school environment that expects them to sit quietly, be docile, polite, and please the teacher. While girls are often treated "with kid gloves," boys are often treated harshly. (In my children's case, if they are both late to homeroom, my son is sent to the office where a large, intimidating assistant principal treats him like a juvenile delinquent. My daughter's lateness is overlooked.) School won't be improved if teachers treat all students the way many boys are treated.

Minority boys and boys from lower socioeconomic groups, in particular, do not fare well in our schools. Contemporary theorists attribute this, at least partly, to "cultural discontinuity."[26] The school culture may be incompatible for these boys because of both cultural and gender differences. Teachers are likely to be Anglo-American women, creating an alien climate for minority boys or boys from lower socioeconomic groups. When students' culture is different from the prevailing school culture, teachers and students clash and confront each other. Teachers misunderstand, misinterpret, and demean students whose behavior they don't understand. Minority boys or boys from lower socioeconomic groups may respond by rejecting school authority and values. Middle-class, Anglo-American boys suffer from less cultural discontinuity and benefit from extra attention and high expectations from their teachers.

Among minority groups, girls often experience much more academic success than boys. Margaret Gibson suggests that girls, socialized to be more passive, may find it easier to accept the school authority and culture. Minority boys may feel more peer pressure to resist Anglo-American, middle-class school values. Acquiescing to the dominant group may be seen as a weakness or as a rejection of their own group.[27]

The situation for minority boys and for all girls is similar in that teachers expect less from them, interact less with them, and send them "low-ability" messages. The situation is very different, however, in that for Anglo-American girls, there is rarely any cultural discontinuity with school. This is, at least partly, why Anglo-American girls tend to make better grades in school. The discontinuity for girls comes later, when they enter the world of work. There they find the female (school) culture and values to be inappropriate to the male-dominated "real world." It is at this point that girls fall behind. The skills and attitudes that girls learned in the schools don't prepare them adequately for the "real world."

Boys (at least Anglo-American ones) who make it successfully through the school system seem better prepared than girls to succeed in the highly competitive adult world. This may be partly because they do not fully accept school socialization. The differential treatment of girls and boys has some high costs for both sexes. Boys are sometimes cocky and unwilling to appreciate their role in failure. They may blame others and therefore not learn from their mistakes. They may set unrealistically high goals which set them up for feelings of failure. Middle-class American society in general is not very forgiving of men who fail to achieve career success.

In the 1960s and 1970s, educators were justifiably concerned about the way that boys were educated. Myra Sadker, David Sadker, and Susan Klein quote one 1965 magazine article: "Boys and the school seem locked in a deadly and ancient conflict that may eventually inflict mortal wounds on both . . . . The problem is not just that teachers are too often women. It is that the school is too much a woman's world, governed by women's rules and standards."[28] Boys' lower grades and disciplinary problems were cited as evidence of an obvious bias against boys. But research starting in the mid 1970s showed that while girls received higher grades in exchange for conforming to school rules, boys got more attention and more active instruction. Teachers worked hard at keeping boys involved and allowed them dominant positions in the classroom. This extra attention was often purely pragmatic classroom management: calling on boys frequently forced them to attend to the lesson. Girls were attentive without extra attention from teachers.

At the same time that some researchers were identifying boys' extra learning opportunities, others were finding out more about the influence of classroom interactions on self-esteem and motivation. It's now clear that schools need to change so that all children have the opportunity to achieve more. Learning techniques to build academic self-confidence, give effective feedback, encourage persistence, and help students set challenging goals will result in improved education for both girls and boys.

As we discuss gender-related issues, it's important to remember that every child's experience and personality is unique; not every girl will fit this book's descriptions and not every boy will be like the "typical" boy described here. The differences among all girls are much greater than the differences between the "average" girl and the "average" boy. The behaviors and attitudes discussed are those on which researchers have found consistent differences, *on the average,* between boys and girls. Just as the average IQ of 100 doesn't describe all children, the descriptions in this book will not apply equally to all children. Teachers and parents should simply look for the patterns described here. We don't want to replace the "old" sex-role stereotypes with new ones; rather, the goal is to help teachers identify and deal with behaviors and attitudes that occur with some frequency, particularly among girls.

We will also be discussing ethnic and cultural differences. Again, it's important not to take descriptions presented here and use them as stereotypes of those groups. The variations in attitudes and behavior within any ethnic group are very large and any one behavior or attitude is never unique to a particular group. For example, while peer rejection of school values is often a problem among African-American boys, not all African-American boys share the problem—and it's certainly not a phenomenon limited to African-American boys. Similarly, despite general beliefs, there are many Asian-American parents who do not particularly encourage high achievement and many non–Asian-American parents who do. The examples used here are to aid in diagnostic and instructional purposes and are not meant to represent the attitudes or behavior of a whole group. We would do well to heed Maria Matute-Bianchi's advice: "It would be a gross misinterpretation . . . to develop specific interventions and programs to 'fit' the modal characteristics of the students I have identified by the typology. A more appropriate response . . . would be to stop creating special programs to fit stereotypic perceptions of students and their perceived problems and to begin changing the school climate, structure and practices to ones that are more broadly sensitive, responsible and challenging to this diverse student clientele."[29]

As we begin talking about achieving gender equity, there's another trap to avoid. Some people argue that for true equity to exist, girls and women should make choices in the same proportion as boys and men. For example, each profession should have 50 percent males and 50 percent females. Or, if 15 percent of boys take calculus in high school; 15 percent of girls should, too. But why should males (usually Anglo-American males) be the yardstick by which females measure themselves?[30] It may be the case that because of women's experiences, they may be more interested in becoming elementary school teachers than men are. As long as each girl is allowed and encouraged to make her own choices, we should not be distressed if her choices follow traditional feminine interests. Nor should we be distressed if boys' choices follow traditional feminine interests. Even if we were to achieve complete equality in the socialization process, we might still find gender differences. Even with complete equality, slightly more males than females may want to become engineers or pilots and more females than males may choose to be full-time homemakers.

Numerical inequity is not the problem. The real problem is *not* that women are more likely to become teachers or nurses and less likely to become pilots, but that traditional female jobs are undervalued. It's a problem if women or men lack choices. While working to allow girls more choices, we need to more highly value the choices that women make. Encouraging girls doesn't mean encouraging them to become like boys. It means encouraging them to explore all options and encouraging them to develop the skills that will give them broad choices. It also means supporting them in the choices they make.

Ensuring equal opportunity doesn't mean blurring gender identity or rejecting all aspects of femininity. Part of being a psychologically healthy person includes a strong sense of identity and that includes a strong *gender identity*. Boys need to know what it means to be a man and to feel good about becoming men. Girls need to look forward to becoming women and feel that being female is a good thing. But just as they have never limited men's options, procreation and childrearing need no longer define women's roles in life. In earlier times, with shorter life expectancies, larger families, and limited educational and career opportunities, childrearing was the dominant role in many women's lives. Now, with longer life spans and fewer children, pregnancy and childrearing take up a smaller proportion of women's lives. With over 60 percent of all mothers of school-age children working outside the home, many women's identities include who they are in the workplace, not just whose wife or mother they are. Being a parent is now a choice, and some women will choose not to have children. Women have time and energy for serious pursuits beyond the home. Today's women have a much wider range of choices and roles than ever before. Girls need to be well prepared to make sound decisions about how to combine the various roles that they may choose for themselves.

Too often young girls are led to believe they can easily do it all and have it all. High school girls often have little awareness of the difficulty of combining career and family. Some, for example, plan high-powered careers, yet believe they can drop out for a few years to have children, not appreciating that with rapidly advancing knowledge, being out of the profession for several years will leave them far behind their colleagues. Encouraging young girls to reach their full potential must also include helping them establish realistic goals and good decision-making skills, as well as being sure they have an academic background that will prepare them for a wide range of options. The head of the Society for Neuroscience's Committee on the Status of Women, Mary Beth Hatten, says "The ideal goal is not to make the career paths of women look precisely like those of men, but rather to equalize opportunities for women and extend to more men the freedom women now feel to choose alternative routes. We don't want to just make women into men, but to broaden the system, to accommodate different styles. The name of the game is freedom."[31] She's right; we need to change the classroom climate so that both girls and boys will feel confident about themselves as young scholars and ready to face academic and life challenges. The problem is not that to be female is "not as good" as to be male, but that our socialization practices place girls at a disadvantage. Today's world requires more flexibility—men and women both need a wide range of interaction styles and a broad array of skills. Both men and women need self-confidence, high levels of motivation, and environments in which they can all learn effectively.

In this book, we will focus on strategies that work well for both girls and boys—strategies that send positive messages to help students learn to persist on challenging tasks and to enjoy learning. Teachers need to monitor the feedback they give and the example that they set as well. In the next section, we will discuss some of the typical ways in which socialization practices differ for boys and girls. As you read this section, think about your own upbringing and about children you know now. See whether you can identify other examples on your own.

Comments on "Emily Butler" and Her Students (from page 11)

1. The first thing Emily Butler said about Monica related to her appearance. This is not necessarily bad, but would it be the first thing that came to mind about a male student? Girls are often rewarded for their appearance rather than for their behavior or performance.

2. Monica, like many girls, is avoiding a risk and not taking a challenging course.

3. It's nice that she is eager to please and works hard, but Emily perceives that as being a "perfect" student. What about creativity, willingness to take risks and accept challenges, and independence? Emily may be unconsciously encouraging girls to be passive and docile.

4. Emily describes what most teachers do—they call on boys more. Emily does this to improve classroom management, but it still has a negative

effect on girls. She needs to find ways to keep students attentive without giving girls less attention.

5. Boys may present more challenges to teachers, but teachers still need to give girls equal learning opportunities. The girls in her class felt less important.

6. The girls in Emily's class wanted to read more about women and more written by women. Emily let her legitimate concerns about boys overshadow the girls' interests and needs. This, too, sends girls the message that their interests are less important.

7. It's great that Emily encouraged girls. We can only hope that she did more than *tell* them they could be anything they wanted to be. She needs to follow through and teach them the necessary skills.

8. As we've learned, excessive praise can sometimes send a "low-ability" message.

9. Monica didn't receive helpful feedback because Emily was afraid of discouraging her. Monica missed the opportunity to learn and improve because Emily handled her with "kid gloves." Paul had the opportunity to learn more because he received more effective feedback.

10. Emily encouraged the girls, but not the boys, to be dependent on her.

11. Once again, Monica shows that she lacks self-confidence and is afraid of a challenge.

ENDNOTES

1. *The National Longitudinal Study of the High School Class of 1972 (NLS-72).* The analyses discussed here come from Clifford Adelman's *Women at Thirtysomething: Paradoxes of Attainment,* U.S. Department of Education, Office of Educational Research and Improvement, June 1991.

2. "Boys Predominate in a Contest, Fueling Complaint of Test Bias," *The New York Times,* May 26, 1993.

3. Katharine and Kermit Hoyenga's (1993) *Gender-related Differences: Origins and Outcomes* (Boston, MA: Allyn and Bacon) offers a thorough and excellent review of gender differences of all types. Diane Halpern's (1986) *Sex Differences in Cognitive Abilities* (Hillsdale NJ: Erlbaum) is another excellent review. For a review of the research on gender differences among high-achieving students, see Carol Mills, Karen Ablard, and Heinrich Stumpf, "Gender Differences in Academically Talented Young

Students' Mathematical Reasoning: Patterns across Age and Subskills," *Journal of Educational Psychology,* 1993, *85,* pp. 340–346.

4. Woolfolk, A. (1993). *Educational Psychology.* Boston, MA: Allyn and Bacon, p. 175.

5. "Women in Science," (Special Section). (1992). *Science, 255,* pp. 1333–1388.

6. Gibbons, Ann, (1992). "Key Issue: Tenure." *Science, 255,* p. 1386.

7. Selvin, P. (1992). "Profile of a Field: Mathematics." *Science, 255,* p. 1383.

8. Ibid., p. 1382.

9. The Wellesley College Center for Research on Women, (1992). *The AAUW Report: How Schools Shortchange Girls.* Washington, D.C.: American Association of University Women Educational Foundation. (Available through AAUW Sales Office, P.O. Box 251, Annapolis Junction, MD 20701-0251.)

10. See Myra Sadker and David Sadker (March 1982), "Sexism in the Classroom: From Grade School to Graduate School," *Phi Delta Kappan,* pp. 513–515, for a nontechnical discussion of some of the major results from recent research. Their (1994) *Failing at Fairness: How America's Schools Cheat Girls* (New York: Charles Schribner's Sons) gives an indepth description and analysis of the problem. For a more scholarly review, see Myra Sadker, David Sadker, and Susan Klein (1991), "The Issue of Gender in Elementary and Secondary Education," in G. Grant (ed.), *Review of Research in Education, 17,* pp. 269–334 Washington, D.C.: American Educational Research Association.

11. Hall, R. M. and Sandler, B. R. (1982). The Classroom Climate: A Chilly One for Women? Washington, D.C.: *Project on the Status and Education of Women,* Association of American Colleges.

12. This section is based on a number of articles about classroom interaction patterns:

> Baker, D. (1986). "Sex Differences in Classroom Interactions in Secondary Science." *Journal of Classroom Interaction, 22,* pp. 212–218.
>
> Bank, B., Biddle, B., and Good, T. (1980). "Sex Roles, Classroom Instruction, and Reading Achievement." *Journal of Educational Psychology, 72,* pp. 119–132.
>
> Boersma, P., Gay, D., Jones, R., and Morrison, L. (1981). "Sex Differences in College Student–Teacher Interactions: Fact or Fantasy?" *Sex Roles, 7,* pp. 775–784.
>
> Brophy, J. (1985). "Interactions of Male and Female Students with Male and Female Teachers." In L. Wilkinson and C. Marrett (eds.), *Gender Influence in Classroom Interactions.* Orlando, FL: Academic Press.
>
> Cherry, L. (1975). "The Preschool Teacher–Child Dyad: Sex Differences in Verbal Interaction." *Child Development, 46,* pp. 532–535.

Clarricoates, K. (1981). "The Experience of Patriarchal Schooling." *Interchange on Educational Policy, 12*, pp. 185–205.

Cornbleth, C., and Korth, W. (1980). "Teacher Perceptions and Teacher–Student Interaction in Integrated Classrooms." *Journal of Experimental Education, 48*, pp. 259–263.

Croll, P. (1985). "Teacher Interaction with Individual Male and Female Pupils in Junior-age Classrooms." *Educational Research, 27*, pp. 220–223.

Erickson, G., and Farkas, S. (1991). "Prior Experience and Gender Differences in Science Achievement." *Alberta Journal of Educational Research, 37*, pp. 225–239.

Fagot, B. I. (1981). "Male and female teachers: Do they treat boys and girls differently?" *Sex Roles: A Journal of Research, 7*, pp. 263–271.

French, J. (1984). "Gender Imbalances in the Primary Classroom: An Interactional Account." *Educational Research, 26*, pp. 127–136.

Good, T., Sikes, J., and Brophy, J. (1973). "Effects of Teacher Sex and Student Sex on Classroom Interactions." *Journal of Educational Psychology, 65*, pp. 74–87.

Good, T., et al. (1980). "Classroom Interaction as a Function of Teacher Expectation, Student Sex, and Time of Year." *Journal of Educational Psychology, 72*, pp. 378–385.

Honig, A. S., and Wittmer, D. S. (1982). "Teacher Questions to Male and Female Toddlers." *Early Child Development and Care, 9*, pp. 19–32.

Irvine, J. (1985). "Teacher Communication Patterns as Related to the Race and Sex of the Student." *Journal of Educational Research, 78*, pp. 338–345.

Jones, M. (1989). "Gender Issues in Teacher Education." *Journal of Teacher Education, 49*, pp. 33–38.

Karp, D., and Yoels, W. (1976). "The College Classroom: Some Observations on the Meaning of Student Participation." *Sociology and Social Research, 60*, pp. 421–439.

Krupnik, C. (1985). "Women and Men in the Classroom." *On Teaching and Learning, 12*, pp. 18–25.

Leinhardt, G. (1979). "Learning What's Taught: Sex Differences in Instruction." *Journal of Educational Psychology, 71*, pp. 432–439.

Rakow, L. (1991). "Gender and Race in the Classroom: Teaching Way Out of Line." *Feminist Teacher, 6*, pp. 10–13.

Sadker, M., and Sadker, D. (1982) "Sexism in the Classroom: From Grade School to Graduate School." *Phi Delta Kappan, 68*, p. 512.

Serbin, L., O'Leary, K., Kent, R., and Tonick, I. (1973). "A Comparison of Teacher Response to the Pre-Academic and Problem Behavior of Boys and Girls." *Child Development, 44*, pp. 796–804.

      Sternglanz, S., and Lyberger-Ficek, S. (1977). "Sex Differences in Student–Teacher Interactions in the College Classroom." *Sex Roles*, pp. 345–352.

      Wilkinson, L., and Marrett, C. (eds.) (1985). *Gender Influences in Classroom Interaction*. Orlando, FL: Academic Press.

13. *AAUW Report*, pp. 70–71.

14. Sadker, M. Sadker, D., and Klein S. (1991). "The Issue of Gender in Elementary and Secondary Education." In G. Grant (ed.), *Review of Research in Education 17*. Washington, D.C.: American Educational Research Association.

15. Gilligan, C. (1982). *In a Different Voice: Psychological Theory and Women's Development*. Cambridge, MA: Harvard University Press; and Brown, L., and Gilligan, C. (1992). *Meeting at the Crossroad: Women's Psychology and Girl's Development* Cambridge: Harvard University Press.

16. Brown and Gilligan (1992), p. 2.

17. Sadker, Sadker, and Klein (1991).

18. *The AAUW Report*.

19. Dweck, C. (1989). "Motivation." In A. Lesgold and R. Glaser (eds.), *Foundations for a Psychology of Education*. Hillsdale, NJ: Lawrence Erlbaum Associates.

20. For more information on gifted girls, see the 1989 (vol. 12) Special Issue of the *Journal for the Education of the Gifted*.

21. Sadker, Sadker, and Klein (1991); Hall and Sandler (1982).

22. Sadker, Sadker, and Klein (1991); Hall and Sandler (1982).

23. For a summary of this literature, see the 1982 (vol. 8) Special Issue of *Sex Roles* on sex differences in causal attributions for success and failure. The following articles are also good sources:

      Campbell, J. (1991). "The Roots of Gender Inequity in Technical Areas." *Journal of Research in Science Teaching, 28,* pp. 251–264.

      Roberts, T. (1991). "Gender and the Influence of Evaluations on Self-Assessments in Achievement Settings." *Psychological Bulletin, 109,* pp. 297–308.

      Ryckman, D., and Peckham, P. (1987). "Gender Differences in Attributions for Success and Failure Situations Across Subject Area." *Journal of Educational Research, 81,* pp. 120–125.

      Stipek, D., and Gralinski, J. (1991). "Gender Differences in Children's Achievement-related Beliefs and Emotional Responses to Success and Failure in Mathematics." *Journal of Educational Psychology, 83,* pp. 361–371.

      Tapasak, R. (1990). "Differences in Expectancy-Attribution Patterns of Cognitive Components in Male and Female Math Performance." *Contemporary Educational Psychology, 15,* pp. 284–298.

24. Dweck, C. (1989). "Motivation." In A. Lesgold and R. Glaser (eds.), *Foundations for a Psychology of Education*. Hillsdale, NJ: Lawrence Erlbaum Associates.

25. Sadker, Sadker, and Klein (1991).

26. Irvine, J. J. (1991). *Black Students and School Failure: Policies, Practices, and Prescriptions*. New York: Praeger.

27. Gibson, M. (1991). "Minorities and Schooling: Some Implications." In M. A. Gibson and J. U. Ogbu's (eds.), *Minority Status and Schooling*. See also J. J. Irvine's (1991) *Black Students and School Failure*, New York: Praeger, for some excellent ideas for dealing with African-American students who are at risk for failure.

28. Sadker, Sadker, and Klein (1991), p. 270.

29. Matute-Bianchi, M. E. (1991). "Situational Ethnicity and Patterns of School Performance among Immigrant and Nonimmigrant Mexican-Descent Students." In M. A. Gibson and J. U. Ogbu (eds.) *Minority Status and Schooling: A Comparative Study of Immigrant and Involuntary Minorities*. New York: Garland Publishing Co., p. 243.

30. See Carol Tavris, *The Mismeasure of Woman* (New York: Simon & Schuster, 1992), for a fascinating history of the way in which the social sciences have mismeasured women by taking men as the standard.

31. Barinaga, M. (1992). "Profile of a Field: Neuroscience." *Science, 255,* p. 1367.

2 | Millie and Willie Grow Up

It's not just the big things, it's also the little, seemingly insignificant things that happen over and over again that make growing up different for boys and girls. These myriad, often indirect, influences comprise the socialization process, and socialization is what underlies gender inequity. We are all products of our socialization, and we *all* treat girls and boys differently.

Consider the following situation. Your friend introduces you to her twelve-year-old child, Chris. Chris is a fresh-faced preadolescent with short hair, dressed in jeans, a bulky sweatshirt and running shoes. You feel awkward because you're not sure whether Chris is a girl or a boy! Why is this situation so uncomfortable? It's because all of us—no matter how liberated—treat girls and boys differently. We don't know how to behave toward Chris. There are societal differences in expectations, attitudes, and behavior that are all part of the socialization process.

Let's start from the beginning and consider two hypothetical children: twins named Millie and Willie. We'll trace their development as examples of what typically happens to girls and boys in our society. Millie and Willie have loving parents who want the best for them. Millie, at birth, has a pink bow glued to her forehead. Willie, who weighs all of an ounce more than his sister, doesn't get the bow. Instead the hospital staff talk about what a big, strong boy he is and how he will be terrorizing his sister in a few years. Friends and relatives send gifts—frilly dresses for Millie and little suits for Willie. His parents laugh at the idea of a fly in his rubber pants, but they will soon learn the "rules" for boy and girl clothes. While boy clothes might have puppies on them, they never have kittens. Balloons are all right for little boy clothes, but flowers aren't. Lace on the collars is a definite "no-no" for boys. Boys' collars are pointed, girls' are round. And of course, boys can never wear pink, but girls can wear blue. There's no rhyme or reason, but everyone follows the rules.

FAMILIES AND EARLY EXPERIENCES

The babies' father, Bill, gets a squirt in the face during his early attempts at changing Willie's diaper. He and Jill, the mother, learn to change Willie's diaper quickly to avoid this problem. Millie, however, doesn't present the danger of a squirt in the face. As a result, like caregivers everywhere, Bill and Jill spend more time playing and interacting with their girl during changing time. They talk and sing to Millie, and Millie learns her first lesson of "conversation" as she responds with her own vocalizations. While this is just one small example of the ways in which parents unintentionally treat girls and boys differently, the implications are staggering. Each baby gets ten to twenty diaper changes per day for two to three years, and girls get an extra sixty seconds of high-quality, face-to-face social interaction each time. That adds up to several hundred extra hours. But more importantly, Millie is learning to attend to and seek out that social interaction. Social interaction becomes more salient and rewarding and hence *all* social interactions become richer opportunities for learning for her. And, the adults are learning that social interaction is more rewarding with Millie than with Willie. So that "little" difference gets magnified and generalized to other situations, each of which interacts with and affects still other situations. Socialization is made up of many, many such small and very natural differences, few of which are based on overt sexism. Diaper changing is just one seemingly trivial example, but it illustrates dramatically how a small difference in behavior can affect many other behaviors.

Let's consider some other examples of parental behavior. Bill plays more roughly with the babies than Jill would like, but she allows more rough and tumble play with Willie. Bill's time with the babies is more often playtime, while Jill does more of the routine caregiving and discipline. When the babies become toddlers, Bill sometimes gives them treats even though Jill doesn't approve of snacks before dinner. Both children learn that it's more fun to play with Daddy and that it seems to be more fun to be a daddy than a mommy.

Jill and Bill are careful to buy gender-neutral toys. They find, however, that toy preferences and play behavior are hard to change. The twins get a punching BoBo Doll for their third birthday. Willie loves punching it and watching it pop back up. Millie sits it in the highchair and pretends to feed it. Willie crashes toy cars; Millie drives them to the store. Millie cuddles her Raggedy Ann; Willie uses his Raggedy Andy as a crash dummy in his Big Wheels. Jill and Bill refuse to buy war toys, so Willie uses sticks for guns. Millie usually chooses typical "girl" toys while Willie usually chooses typical "boy" toys. Boys' toys and activities tend to require active play and problem solving. Girls' toys elicit more role-play and quieter play. Boys' games usually have winners and losers; girls' rarely do. Some girls in the twins' playgroup are a little more active and aggressive than Millie and often play with the boy toys. Their fathers laugh and call them "little tomboys." But like most little girls, Millie is Daddy's "little doll" and his interactions with her are more likely to involve tea parties than rough and tumble play.

Not only are there girl toys and boy toys, but there are girl Saturday-morning cartoons and boy Saturday-morning cartoons. The characters and the storylines are very different and reflect sex-role stereotypes ("Baby Sitter Club" versus "Teenage Ninja Turtles"). Petra Hesse and Susan Cross have analyzed the content of these programs[1] and characterize the slogan for boy cartoons as, "Let's reach out and crush someone," while the slogan for girl cartoons is more like, "Let your heart be your guide." In the boys' shows, heroes win by violent and aggressive actions. The girls' heroes defend themselves with rainbows, magic, and kindness. Girls' stories take place in magical, fantasy places such as Care-o-Lot and Smurf Village. Boys' stories involve political enemies—Nazis, Soviets, Arabs, or space aliens. After the average preschooler watches twenty-five to thirty hours of television each week, it's not surprising that girls will be more likely to see themselves as powerless and dependent on magic or a man to rescue them. Boys learn that violence and aggression are effective means of conflict resolution. Millie and Willie also each begin to choose sex-appropriate books, which again differ in emphasis and reflect sex-role stereotypes.

Willie and Millie each has a distinct personality, but even when they behave in the same way, their behavior is perceived differently. In one research study, subjects were shown a picture of a baby crying.[2] The subjects who were told that the baby was a boy said he was crying because he was mad; subjects told it was a girl said she was crying because she was afraid. Similarly, Millie and Willie's behavior is "interpreted," and this interpretation is influenced by the child's sex. People expect Willie to act like a boy (always into something, super-active, independent, more likely to get dirty) and Millie to act like a girl (quieter, less active, timid, dependent, more social). Willie and Millie's parents, like others studied by researchers, are unaware that they have different expectations and reactions to their children.[3] They are smug in their belief that their children are being raised in a nonsexist environment.

PEERS AND PLAY

By preschool, children already have strong preferences for same-sex playmates. At four-and-a-half-years of age, they spend nearly three times as much time with same-sex playmates as with playmates of the other sex.[4] By the time they are six-and-a-half, they are spending eleven times as much time with same-sex playmates. Although preschool children's play is sex-segregated, many of their activities are gender-neutral. Both girls and boys enjoy the housekeeping center, blocks, trucks, and role-play.

But even in early childhood, play differs dramatically in boys' versus girls' groups. Eleanor Maccoby believes children's early play groups are a primary source of lessons in how males and females should act.[5] She reports strikingly similar patterns of gender differences throughout life. Boys' groups tend to be rowdier. Their play takes up more space and therefore is often out of doors or in public places. Girls' play tends to be more intimate and often takes place in more private places. Males have a more *restrictive* verbal style that inhibits interaction. Boys threaten, brag, interrupt, or do other things that inhibit further talk. Girls' verbal interactions are more *enabling* or *facilitating*. Girls do things to keep the conversation—and the relationship—going. They listen more, agree with what others have said, or offer support. Girls use this more facilitative style to influence each other. Boys influence each other in more direct ways; they may tell somebody what to do or use physical force. Girls influence others in more indirect ways. Boys worry about establishing dominance, especially when other boys are watching. Just as in the animal kingdom, human males establish dominance hierarchies and mark their territory. Maccoby believes that the male obsession for dominance and turf makes it important for males not to show weakness in front of other males. This, she argues, may be the reason for their more restrictive interaction style. Because girls' play is less public and usually in smaller groups, they have less to lose by being more facilitative.

Deborah Tannen gives some fascinating examples of early conversations that clearly demonstrate these differences.[6] In a daycare center, Lisa wanted Mary's plastic pickle. Sue intervened on Lisa's behalf. Here's how the girls dealt with the problem.

Mary: I cut it in half. One for Lisa, one for me, one for me.
  Sue: But, Lisa wants a *whole* pickle!
Mary: Well, it's a whole *half* pickle.
  Sue: No, it isn't.
Mary: Yes, it is, a whole *half* pickle.
  Sue: *I'll* give her a whole half. I'll give her a *whole whole.* I gave her a whole one.

Sue then pretends to give Lisa a "whole whole" pickle.

Three boys later fought over the same plastic pickle. Notice their different interaction style.

Nick: [Screams] Kevin, but the, oh, I *have* to cut! I want to cut it! It's mine!

Nick then involved a third child to help him secure the pickle.

Nick: [Whining to Joe] Kevin is not letting me cut the pickle.
Joe: Oh, I know! I can pull it away from him and give it back to you. That's an idea![7]

Both Kevin and Lisa wanted the pickle, but they went about trying to get their way very differently. The girls tried compromise and evasion; the boys tried physical force. In other conversations reported by Tannen, girls expressed preferences and suggestions while boys were more apt to give orders "Gimme!" or "Get outta here!" When playing doctor, boys said "Lie down," or "Gimme your arm." Girls suggested, "Let's sit down and use this." In fact, many of the conversations among little girls that Tannen reports start with "Let's."

Gender differences in behavior are much more pronounced in mixed-sex groups.[8] Girls are much more likely to be passive, for example, when with boys than when in all-girl groups. (Indeed, this is one of the arguments for all-women colleges: women assume more leadership roles and are more assertive if no men are around.) Maccoby argues that it's unlikely that girls learn to assume a passive role mostly through early family interactions. Differential behavior depending on the gender composition of groups shows up very early—when children are less than three years old. Girls this age probably don't view their two-year-old male playmates as "like Daddy" and their two-year-old female playmates as "like Mommy." Children this age are more likely to see adults as another species altogether. They don't expect little children (their peers) to behave much like adults of either sex. Further, in most families with small children, mothers are pretty powerful people. Even if the father makes the "big" decisions and earns more money, most mothers control the daily lives of small children. Mothers are more likely to decide when and what to eat, how to behave, what activities are available, when to nap, and so forth. Children often believe that Mommy has all the money, because they are much more likely to see mothers spend money. Even in families in which child care is shared equally and fathers are involved in daily care, mothers are not lacking influence nor do they appear passive to their young children. To most two- and three-year-olds, mommies are at least as powerful as, if not more powerful than, daddies. Further, if girls learn to let boys dominate through observing family interactions, then it's hard to explain why girls with younger brothers or no brothers behave just like girls with older brothers. Surely younger brothers are less likely to dominate sisters than are older brothers. So where do girls learn to allow boys to dominate? Maccoby suggests that they learn it from boys. Girls learn that boys play rough and don't listen to girls. They learn that they can have more influence in all-girl groups. Parents no doubt contribute by supporting same-sex playgroups and by allowing boys to be rough and domineering. Maccoby argues that these lessons are most likely learned from interacting with *peers* and not from observing parents or other adults.

Organized play differs, too, for girls and boys. Willie and Millie play soccer. (Their parents, after all, believe in gender equity and want Millie to learn about teamwork.) The coach of the boys' team yells at Willie when he makes mistakes and stresses competition. The coach of the girls' team focuses on everyone having a good time and emphasizes the positive. When the boys make an error, the coach goes over the mistake so that they learn from it. The girls' coach praises them for already perfected skills and attends less to their skill deficits. The girls' coach praises everyone. The boys learn that praise and criticism are directly related to their performance. After a game, the girls ask their coach and parents, "How did we do?" A boy knows how he did.

When my own children were little, I was struck by how coaches treat even quite young boys. My son, at age 7, was publicly dressed down when the other team scored while he was playing goalie. I realized that no one in my entire life had ever treated me that harshly. The coach explained to me afterwards that if "he wants to be good, he's got to be able to take the heat." Boys are often put under intense, competitive pressure. Those who learn "to take the heat" do well later in life, while those who "can't take the heat" are in for trouble. Girls who are never exposed to the heat also may be unprepared for the highly competitive nature of many careers.

LIFE AT SCHOOL

Willie and Millie go to a progressive nursery school, yet their daily lives differ. Teachers interact more with boys, although this is largely due to the need to supervise and control their behavior.[9] Girls receive more recognition for good behavior. Deborah Tannen gives the following example of a kindergarten teacher talking to her students:

Oh my, what a nice-looking group of kindergartners. Oh, it makes Mrs. Bedford so happy to see such smiling faces. Now, are we all sitting comfortably? [*Pause*] Let's see who is here. Looks like everybody's here. Our line leader for today is Mark W. [*Students talking among themselves.*] Oh, I like the way Tammy and Barbara are sitting down. They're so ready for first grade. Oh, and Corrie and Heather, how nice . . . and Colleen and Sherrie, you look terrific. Joey, could you turn around so I can see your face? Steven T., would you come sit up here by me? Bobby, find a place there. Stephen S., right there is a good place for you. Is everybody comfortable? Are we ready?[10]

Notice that the girls are complimented for their good behavior and the boys are mildly and indirectly criticized for not "sitting nicely." Other, less "progressive" teachers might have been more direct with the boys, perhaps yelling at them to behave. Teachers talk to girls and boys differently even when classroom management is not at stake. Girls are asked more personal–social questions.[11] For example, Millie might be asked where she got her pretty curls or about her feelings, while Willie might be asked about classroom activities.

Most of these differences are unconscious, and teachers are unaware of differences in the questions that they ask girls versus boys. I still catch myself, when asking my teenage children how their school day went, asking my daughter about people and relationships and asking my son more about the content of his courses.

In the classroom, boys receive more attention. The male/female discrepancy in teacher interaction becomes greater as the teacher's comments become more specific.[12] So when Willie makes an error, the teacher not only responds, but gives him more extensive and specific feedback. When Willie doesn't answer a question immediately, the teacher waits or gives him hints. When Millie doesn't answer immediately, the teacher calls on someone else. Willie calls out answers without raising his hand, and the teacher accepts his answer, even praises him sometimes. If Millie speaks without raising her hand, she is reprimanded. In science class, Willie commandeers the lab equipment, while Millie tends to watch her male lab partner. When Willie makes a mistake, the teacher is more likely to tell him to work hard; when Millie errs, the teacher is more likely to imply she lacks ability.

By the time they start elementary school, Willie and Millie already have well-developed styles of interacting, and have their own interest patterns. They also have different bodies of knowledge. They've read different books and watched different television shows. They've played different games. They've played in different groups. Willie knows more than Millie about certain sports and vehicles of all kinds. Millie is an expert on Barbie dolls. Millie has a bigger vocabulary; Willie is better at puzzles. They are hardly "empty vessels" waiting to be filled by teachers. Their teachers react to the real differences that exist as well as those seen through the "eye of the beholder." The older the children become, the more their interests and knowledge bases diverge. At the same time that the children are becoming more sex-typed, adults (often unconsciously) are differentially expecting, responding to, and interpreting differences in behaviors and attitudes. This results in a spiraling effect, with gender differences escalating.

Children strongly prefer to play in same-sexed groups, but when Millie and Willie's teachers form mixed work groups, an interesting thing happens. When the teacher is nearby, boys allow girls more of a chance to talk and they even listen some to what girls have to say. But when the teacher moves away, the boys take over and the girls are put in submissive roles. The teacher's presence apparently inhibits the boys' more dominant and powerful interaction style.[13] It's difficult to change students' preferences for same-sex groups, but Maccoby reports that children can and do work well in mixed groups when under close supervision by an adult and when there is an engaging, mutual task. Marlaine Lockheed reports that after exposure to mixed-sex working groups, fourth- and fifth-grade boys actually preferred mixed groups.[14] This means that teachers, as the adults who supervise groups, can significantly alter what girls learn from peer group interaction. If, as Maccoby argues, social groups are one of the main vehicles by which girls learn disadvantageous behavior patterns, then restructuring social groups is one way to equalize opportunities. Teachers are the people most capable of reformulating group interactions. Strategy 11 in Chapter 3 offers some suggestions on how teachers can use groups to broaden the range of students' interaction skills.

Willie and the other little boys tease the girls unmercifully. When Millie and the other girls cry or complain to the teacher, the teacher laughs and says, "Boys will be boys." Millie notices that when children tease Sam, the boy in the wheelchair, the teacher tells them that it's wrong to embarrass him or to hurt his feelings. One day a group of Anglo-American boys make fun of an African-American boy and the teacher delivers a long lecture on respecting others. Millie wonders why it's okay to be mean to girls. Even her parents don't take it seriously when Willie teases her or hurts her feelings. (Remember the hospital staff who predicted Willie would soon be "terrorizing his sister"?)

Sue Askew and Carol Ross have developed and taught a antisexist course for boys in London.[15] Among the things they documented in their study of mixed-sex classrooms is a high level of harassment of girls at all grade levels, both physically and verbally. They argue that this on-going intimidation is a means of proving masculinity, an activity that teachers accept as legitimate. They report that teachers "talked about their determination not to respond" to the harassment. Teachers apparently feel that such behavior is best ignored.

The harassment that girls experience at school continues through high school and can be intense. The AAUW report included results from an extensive study of sexual harassment in school. Both boys and girls reported unpleasant verbal and physical harassment starting in early grades. Boys who don't live up to their peers' narrow definitions of masculinity are often the target of abuse. Girls seem to be targeted simply for being girls. Many girls reported debilitating cases of sexual harassment. *Seventeen* magazine recently documented the extreme pain that some girls experience at school.[16] In almost all cases, girls report that it is difficult to get teachers to take their concerns seriously. Schools tolerate a great deal of unkindness toward girls that would never be tolerated against any other group of students. Children learn early that society allows females to be harassed.

The patterns that are laid down as early as preschool seem to persist throughout the school years and into adulthood. Later, in the workplace, men tend to focus more on tasks while women focus more on relationships.[17] Men engage in more task-related behavior, such as giving information, directions, suggestions, and opinions. Women are more likely to behave in ways that facilitate relationships within the group. In one study, when asked what they had learned from the "school of hard knocks," male executives talked about technical lessons, female executives cited lessons about people.[18] It's not far-fetched to argue that this difference results from early socialization—remember that girls learn that diaper changing is about social interaction while boys learn it's a task to be accomplished as quickly and efficiently as possible.

As adults, male voices are louder, plus men have learned to interrupt more and to tell people directly what to do. The same pattern is evident in Willie and Millie's preschool classroom. Is it surprising that males are more likely to command attention? Females who wait for a turn to speak may not get a turn. While agreeing with other speakers works well in all-female groups and usually results in some reciprocity, it is usually interpreted as yielding to males in mixed groups. Both male and female ways of interacting are legitimate and indeed, useful. The problem stems from males' dominant style. Women's style often gets overshadowed and they are left in the background. Returning to Millie and Willie, girls in mixed-gender groups—little girls as well as big girls—find it difficult to influence boys and find themselves as passive participants, looking on as boys do things.

These patterns, however, are not immutable. In situations where power has been equalized, women's interaction styles more closely resemble men's. When a woman has the legitimate role of "boss," she can be more forceful and dominant in her interactions. In classrooms, too, if girls are designated as legitimate leaders and publicly recognized as such, they can be more dominant. Male behavior, too, can change. When men are not competing against each other to establish masculinity or dominance, they become more facilitative in their interactive style. Structuring workgroups so that they have engaging tasks that require cooperation rather than competition and so that girls' leadership roles are clearly defined is one way to break the traditional communication patterns.

FAMILIES AND CULTURE

Among the children in Willie and Millie's class are a range of different family situations and different cultures. The range of ways in which sex roles are played out is enormous. Joe, like about 25 percent of American children today, lives in a single-parent home.[19] Since he was a young boy, Joe has heard his mother and her divorced friends denigrate men. They hang out, discussing their ex-husbands and boyfriends, usually emphasizing men's lack of commitment, unreliability, insensitivity, and other negative attributes. Just as little Joe is trying to figure out what it means to be a man, he is bombarded with very negative perspectives on masculinity. He has few male role models. His mother, from time to time, has a boyfriend. But it seems to Joe that as soon as he becomes attached, the relationship ends. He sees adult men as people who don't stay around and who hurt his mother. He is confused and ambivalent about the male role. It's hard to feel good about yourself if you're a member of such a denigrated group. He particularly feels bad when the teacher suggests "having your fathers help with your science project" or when there's a father–son banquet. Joe has self-esteem and self-confidence problems, as well as academic ones.

Janet also lives with only her mother. Like Joe, she's having some difficulties with sex-role development. She has difficulties interacting with males, and as she enters her teens, she is overly eager to attract boys and becomes promiscuous. Her boy-craziness interferes with her schoolwork, as well as with her long-term plans.

Teachers see many academic as well as social and personal problems that seem to be exacerbated by family situations. And families seem to get more and more complex. In addition to the growing number of emotionally dysfunctional families, teachers see increasingly diverse family structures and wonder how to deal with the complicated sets of parents, stepfamilies, and extra sets of grandparents, not to mention parents with temporary live-ins or gay partners. Even the Hallmark company is overburdened, now with cards for 105 different familial relationships![20] How are students supposed to deal with the explosion of extra relatives?

Even in what appear to be stable two-parent families, often both parents work at stressful, time-consuming jobs that leave little time for the children. Studies show busy parents who both work spend about thirty seconds a day in "meaningful" conversation with their children.[21] Few extended families are available to take up the slack. Students are under more stress than they were a generation ago. In both high- and low-income districts, teachers report getting less parental support and involvement than they'd like. Teachers try hard to help students develop self-confidence and good attitudes toward school, but it's difficult when these lessons are not reinforced in the home and when students have so many nonacademic problems.

Maria's parents have some very different views on what's appropriate for girls and boys than do Millie and Willie's parents.[22] Maria's parents are from Mexico and believe that education is of far less importance to girls. Their expectation for Maria is that she will marry young, raise a large family, and not work outside the home. In junior high, when counselors begin talking to students and parents about college-prep courses, Maria's parents insist that Maria not be in the college track despite her good grades and high standardized test scores. Much to Maria's teacher's dismay, there are other students from various cultural backgrounds whose parents cling to what she considers to be outmoded ideas about women's role. In fact, some parents have complained about a textbook that shows men caring for children and women as firefighters. How can she raise these girls' expectations if their parents believe women's only role is in the home?

Ashley is a bright, attractive child with parents who are deeply concerned about her education. Her parents are pushing her toward engineering and continually remind her that "girls can do anything boys can do." They discouraged her playing with dolls and seem intent on proving to the world that Ashley is more capable than any boy. Ashley, like some other children of pushy parents, is under tremendous pressure to be the best and the brightest. Any observer at Little League is aware of parental pressure on children to compete. *Harper's Magazine* reports that one hundred referees of children's sports activities are attacked by parents each year.[23] Is it little wonder that teachers feel anxious and defensive when dealing with highly competitive parents?

Binyao's parents are first generation from China. First grade is difficult for him; as an only child he is used to constant, individual attention. In Chinese culture, children are encouraged to be more dependent than in middle-class American culture. Consequently, Binyao seems younger than his classmates. His parents have high expectations for Binyao and believe his success will be a matter of pride for his entire family. Any failure will dishonor the family.

Malcolm's parents want him to do well in school. They rarely attend Parent Teacher Association meetings or parent–teacher conferences because of work schedules and the fact that they feel somewhat uncomfortable in the school setting. The teacher, however, mistakenly interprets this in combination with Malcolm's poor academic achievement as evidence that Malcolm's parents, and most impoverished African-American parents, aren't concerned with school. She blames his poor achievement on his family and fails to see any connection between his performance and what goes on in school.[24]

The class also has students from various different socioeconomic classes. Patterns of achievement vary dramatically by social class. One study showed that among eighth-grade girls, those from low socioeconomic classes tend to do better than boys from similar backgrounds. But among high socioeconomic groups, boys do as well as or better than girls. By high school, the boys with a high socioeconomic status do better than girls.[25] Among less educated and less affluent parents, sex roles are often more rigid.[26] Better educated parents encourage more *androgyny* in their children. Sandra Bem defines androgyny as possessing both masculine and feminine characteristics and hence being able to act in typically male or female ways, depending on the demands of a particular situation.[27] Some parents are pleased to have a teacher encourage boys in art, music, and dance; others are horrified and label such interests as "sissy." Social-class differences result in different expectations and beliefs about what's appropriate for boys and girls. (In my own case, I grew up assuming men fixed things. My husband grew up assuming that when appliances or cars broke, women called repairmen. We resolved the conflict by having my husband call repair*persons*.)

As Willie and Millie's teacher looks around her classroom, she's struck by how many students have parents with conflicting ideas, goals, and hang-ups concerning their child's gender-role identity and how these perspectives affect academic achievement. She's amazed, too, at the array of parenting styles. When a "bad" report card is sent home, some parents threaten, some cajole, some punish, some blame themselves, and some ignore the message. Only a few seem to take what the teacher considers to be constructive, corrective steps. How can she help all these very different parents help their children achieve? What's a teacher to do when there's this much diversity?

The diversity is not only in terms of parental values. Students belong to different peer groups, which provide differing levels of support for academic success. Laurence Steinberg, Sanford Dornbusch, and B. Bradford Brown find that ethnic differences in achievement are influenced not only by family values and practices, but also by the interaction of parenting and peer support.[28] For example, African-American parents tend to be more authoritative (stressing self reliance and independence) than authoritarian (stressing obedience to authority), a style which, in general, has positive benefits for achievement. Some African-American adolescent peer groups, however, do not support academic endeavors, which undermines the positive influence of parents' authoritative style. Asian-American parents tend to be more authoritarian, a style which is usually associated with *lower* achievement. But in the case of Asian-American students, peers offer high levels of support that offset any negative consequences of the authoritarian parenting style. Steinberg and his colleagues argue that although "parents are the most salient influence on youngsters' long-term educational plans, peers are the most potent influence on their day-to-day behaviors in school" (p. 727). And of course, the day-to-day behavior is what determines academic performance, which then determines which educational plans the student will have the choice to follow.

"The media sure isn't helping either," moans the teacher. "I try to help my students set realistic, long-term goals, and to appreciate hard work, but every time they turn on the television, they see instant gratification. To look at TV, you'd think nobody has to work for anything. In sitcoms, kids who do well in school are portrayed as nerds. Television only shows the glamour of success; it never shows the hard work and sacrifice. What's more, TV is still full of sexual and racial stereotypes. I only wish there were some way to counteract it."

As Willie and Millie grow up, their peers begin to influence them more and more. Millie wants boys to like her and quickly learns that being "too smart" has some social disadvantages. This is also the point at which her self-esteem begins to drop as she realizes she isn't going to have a figure like her Barbie doll and is not going to be admired for her brain. Adolescence can be traumatic for some boys, too, but in Lyn Mikel Brown and Carol Gilligan's words, for girls (especially middle-class Anglo-American girls) it is a *crossroads*.[29] Girls have learned to place a high value on relationships and getting along with people and as they become older, they learn to silence themselves in order to maintain harmony. They begin to place their own needs and feelings second to those of others. They worry about how others will see (and judge) them. In the process of shifting their focus to how others will view them, girls begin to lose some of their own identity and often some of their self-esteem.

Some of Willie and Millie's African-American and Hispanic-American peers experience other problems with identity and self-confidence. They learn that doing well in school is considered "acting white," and those students who do well in school may face considerable peer pressure to reject school values. How much a student's peer group supports academics is a powerful predictor of how well a student will do. Many ethnic minority students find that racial segregation limits their choices for peer groups. If peer groups that support achievement are more likely to be Anglo-American or Asian-American, then African-American and Hispanic-American teenagers may have difficulty joining these groups, especially if joining them is interpreted as rejecting their ethnic peers. Many African-American students whose parents are highly supportive of academic achievement, and who themselves want to excel academically, find it difficult to join a peer group with that value. Signithia Fordham and John Ogbu report that African-American teenagers are more likely than other students to be torn between performing well in school and being popular with their peers.[30] Teenagers have to juggle often conflicting values of family, school, and peers.

As Millie and Willie enter the teen years, their parents begin to worry more about Millie and an additional double standard for their behavior develops.[31] While it's true that in many ways females are more vulnerable in our society, the twins' parents probably protect Millie more than necessary—they may, for example, set an earlier curfew for her, worry more about her dates, or not let her go out alone. When Willie is caught drinking, his parents are upset. But when *Millie* is caught drinking, they are distraught—nice girls simply don't drink. They worry that Millie may become promiscuous or harm her reputation; Bill takes pride in Willie's being a "ladies' man." Sometimes Millie and her parents feel they're in a time warp; in some ways, everything's changed and girls can "do anything they want." But in other ways, very little has changed. Jacqueline Jackson of the Rhode Island Rape Crisis Center, for example, reports that 22 percent of sixth- to twelfth-grade boys say it's acceptable for a man to rape his date if he "spent a lot of money" on her.[32] The twins' parents don't know how much freedom to give Millie and how much to protect her.

As the twins plan for college, their parents may convey the message that a good education is more important for Willie. Or, they may feel that some fields of study are "better" for one child or the other. Teachers and counselors may give the children very different advice and encouragement. Both children begin exploring scholarships. Millie finds that the number-one source of money for college scholarships for women is national and local Miss America pageants.[33] This reflects a general difference in the children's experience: Millie has been rewarded and praised for more superficial things, such as her appearance, while Willie's rewards have been more often contingent on performance. Willie has had to work to receive praise from teachers, parents, and coaches. Millie has been praised for simply being cute, being nicely dressed, or being quiet. To Willie, reward or praise result from his own abilities or efforts.

Even when the twins go to college, they will be treated differently. Men do more talking in classes. Professors listen more attentively and are more encouraging to men. Professors ask about Willie's future plans but not about Millie's. (When my husband and I were seniors in college, we had nearly identical academic records. His professors offered to write him letters. My professors were happy to write me letters, but I had to ask for their professional support. His advisor urged him to go to graduate school. Mine thought it was a good idea when I brought it up.) Some professors joke about women and even belittle women's accomplishments. The twins see relatively few female professors. Most of the women teachers they have are teaching assistants or temporary instructors; most of the full professors, department chairs, deans and other administrators are men. The vast majority of temporary faculty are women. Millie feels out of place in male-dominated departments such as engineering, physics and math. Willie feels self-conscious in classes such as education or nursing, which are made up mostly of women. Although equally talented in math, Millie doesn't pursue courses beyond the requirements. Although interested in child development, Willie gravitates toward other fields. Nobody tells them they have to do this; it just feels more comfortable. The world looks different to Millie and Willie.[34] On a daily basis, they experience different versions of reality. This process started early in their life and now Willie and Millie, like most men and women, live side by side, yet in different worlds.

STEREOTYPES AND SELECTIVE ATTENTION

The way people process information adds another dimension to the socialization process. We don't just treat boys and girls differently, we also *think* about boys and girls differently. To fully understand this complex process, we need to look at how stereotypes work and at the phenomenon of selective attention. Then we need to see how this all fits together when people set goals.

Teachers, like everyone else, use stereotypes. We all use stereotypes because we are *limited information processors* and need to simplify the mass of incoming data. Stereotypes are really just categories. We naturally categorize information. For example, once I categorize an animal as a mammal, I immediately can infer some of its characteristics. Stereotypes are not inherently bad, but teachers need to be aware of the stereotypes that they do use and minimize the inferences made on the basis of stereotypes. Teachers often jump to conclusions based on a students' sex, social class, ethnic group, or appearance. They need to withhold judgment until they come to know the student.

Stereotypes classify a whole group of people as having the same set of characteristics. Some stereotypical female traits are very positive: women are supposed to be warm and nurturing. The stereotype may even have a grain of truth; on the average, women probably are warmer and more nurturing than men. The stereotype is inaccurate, however, because not *all women* have these traits and because *many men* do have them. The trick is not so much to eliminate the stereotypes as to learn that individuals in the group are not all alike and don't all share the same traits. The goal in the classroom is *not* to convince students that women shouldn't bake cookies and that women should be firefighters. A better goal is to convince students that *some* women and *some* men bake cookies and *some* women and *some* men are firefighters—and therefore, knowing someone's sex is not a good basis for predicting their interests or career.

With no stereotype, we think of people being what statisticians call "normally distributed." If, for example, we have no stereotype of male drivers, we would believe that male drivers vary from awful to highly skilled, with most men being average drivers. If we drew a curve representing this conception of male drivers, it would look like the standard bell-shaped curve (Figure 2.1).

Consider the old (and false!) stereotype: "Women are bad drivers." Someone holding that stereotype would have a different representation for female drivers. Rather than a bell-shaped curve, they'd have all women bunched up at the "poor" end of the scale. To overcome stereotypes, then, we need to convince people that female drivers come in all varieties (just like male drivers). To accomplish this conversion, we need to present lots of female drivers with *varying* skills.

Note that simply presenting female race-car drivers doesn't convince people that women are normally distributed with regard to driving. In fact, what would happen is that the person with the stereotyped ideas would simply figure that there are lots of regular women (bad drivers) and some freaks of nature who are

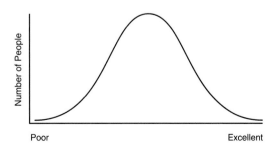

Poor   Excellent

Figure 2.1 Bell-Shaped Curve.

female race-car drivers—the exception that proves the rule. So to change stereotypical thinking, the best strategy is not to present students with extreme examples of women doing highly masculine tasks, but to present them with *lots* of examples of men and women doing a *wide* range of tasks.

Changing stereotypes is difficult. Consider the stereotype of women being bad drivers. Experience doesn't always eliminate prejudice. Because attention is *selective*, people don't notice everything around them. Instead, their attention is captured by things that confirm their beliefs. People see what they expect to see and what they want to see. The person who believes women to be bad drivers notices all the poor female drivers, and fails to notice the good female drivers and the bad male drivers. Over time, the stereotype gets reinforced because all those confirming instances are noticed and the disconfirming ones ignored. When confronted with a clear case of a good female driver, our prejudiced person sees her as an exception—the exception that proves the rule.

What this means for the teacher is that it's not enough to put up a few pictures of women in nontraditional jobs or to have a few stories about women doing nontraditional things. Instead, teachers have to present many examples of both men and women in a wide range of jobs and activities in order to demonstrate effectively that both women and men are normally distributed with regard to talents, abilities, and interests. To really change stereotypes, students need to see more than the exceptional case. The same lesson is important in regard to stereotypes about racial minorities. It's good to have pictures and stories about exceptional minority members who have made superachievements. But to change the stereotypes, show students that minorities come in *all* varieties of ability, just like people in the majority culture. Rather than focusing on a few super role models, try to have as many different people depicted doing as many different things as possible. Don't limit choices to the exotic; try to show average people doing average things. Just be sure to include lots of diversity in the average range. Chapter 3 presents more ideas and exercises to help reduce dependence on stereotypes.

LEARNING VERSUS PERFORMANCE GOALS

Schools focus on goals. Every test, assignment, and grading period represents an opportunity to set a goal. Most school goals are *performance goals;* they focus on how well a teacher thinks the student performed, usually in comparison to other students' performance.[35] Students lack control over important aspects of performance goals. They can't control how the teacher will choose to evaluate them or the other students' performance. Because girls are socialized to be more concerned than boys with pleasing others, girls usually take performance goals very seriously. They really want the teacher to like their performance. In fact, for girls and women, doing a task well is something they often do more to please others than to please themselves. Good work means they are good girls. They want their papers to be good so the teacher will like them personally.

Outside of school, the same pattern remains common. Women want to please the boss so that the boss will like them. Men want to please the boss so that they will get a raise. Women often see tasks as a way to show that they care. Men are more likely to see tasks simply as things that need to be done. (Sounds like diaper changing again?) Women often become more dependent on interpersonal feedback. Thus, a cycle develops. Girls want to do well so teachers will like them; society teaches girls to be more attuned to interpersonal relationships and rewards them more for interpersonal skills than other types of skills; society expects girls to behave and do their homework; women's accomplishments are often undervalued; girls and women are expected to conform; girls are rewarded more for being "nice" than for being smart, and on and on. Good grades confirm to girls that they are okay and that the teacher likes them. The irony is that girls are particularly tuned in to those very cues that then discourage them from achieving.[36]

Girls are supposed to like school more than boys do and they're supposed to do what the teacher expects. When people simply do what is expected, they don't get much special attention. But if someone violates expectations, it must mean something. If girls don't do well, for example, it must be because they're not very smart. Many girls *need* good grades to feel valued. Because girls receive less corrective feedback from teachers, they are not very good at evaluating their own performance. This makes them *need* the external feedback from teachers. Boys are less needy. They are told when they perform poorly. This negative feedback helps them learn to evaluate their own work so they become less dependent on grades to let them know they're okay. As in the soccer example, girls need to be told they're okay; boys know how they did. Boys learn to get satisfaction from the task itself; girls often rely more on feedback from people for satisfaction. High achieving girls get "hooked" on good grades and praise.

Boys are often less concerned about grades and performance goals. We don't expect boys to like school. When boys don't do well, it's presumed to be, at least partly, because they don't like school; it doesn't mean much with regard to their abilities. "Everybody knows" that boys will be boys, and this means they're not as likely to turn in their homework or be neat. A boy who does not make a good grade or do his homework may not be dumb—he may just be behaving like a boy. Remember Paul in Emily Butler's class. He didn't turn in his homework, yet Emily still thought he was bright. Boys aren't as concerned with pleasing the teacher because pleasing the teacher and schoolwork are more "girl" things. Boys do things because they're fun rather than because they're supposed to. Boys are less concerned about school performance and hence academic performance goals.

Another, better kind of goal than a performance goal is a *learning goal*. It's simply a goal to learn something. A student might set a learning goal, for example, to improve her reading skills. Learning goals are under the learner's control: given any minimal effort, a student will learn something. Success toward a learning goal doesn't depend on others' performance or on how the teacher evaluates the performance. With learning goals, you evaluate yourself. Learning goals helps students learn self-evaluation. Because males are often freer to learn things for fun while females often feel they have to do well to gain approval, females are less likely to set learning goals for themselves. Learning goals are good for everyone. They are highly motivating, they are under the student's control, the student is nearly always successful with learning goals, and they teach students to be intrinsically motivated. Teachers need to encourage learning goals for all students; but for girls, teachers need to deemphasize performance goals as well. Learning goals encourage risks; performance goals encourage safety.

Think back to Emily Butler's remarks. Emily, like many teachers, is focusing on learning goals for Paul and performance goals for the girls.

"I went over Paul's paper with a fine-toothed comb. I sure hope he learned grammar from my class. . . . I encouraged Monica and Jessica. I wanted them to know they could get A's."

Now that we've seen the multitude of ways in which girls' and boys' experiences differ, we're ready in Chapter 3 to focus on how teachers can positively influence the socialization process for all students.

This book focuses on how teachers can help girls overcome barriers to achievement. As new research points to differences in teacher behavior and educational climate for boys and girls, it's becoming clear that achieving gender equity is more difficult than ensuring equal sport opportunities, equal opportunity for coursework or even having equal representation of women and girls in children's reading materials. To achieve gender equity, teachers have to change their own attitudes as well as how they teach. A decade ago, a book like this would have stopped with suggestions on changing the curriculum or the classroom materials or perhaps using nonsexist language. But with new research in psychology, we can go further. In today's classrooms, girls are rarely told they can't do math or shouldn't bother to go to college. Textbooks show women and men in both career and nurturing roles. In preschools, little boys play in the housekeeping center and little girls play with trucks and blocks. Women are swelling the ranks of professional schools. Many of the obvious external barriers to women's success have been knocked down (or at least lowered!). Now it's time to focus on some of the *internal barriers* to success. These internal barriers are attitudes, expectations, and fears that result from subtle differences in the way that girls and boys are socialized. While few people today tell girls they can't be engineers or physicians, girls still get subtle and indirect messages that they are not expected to excel in certain areas. Teachers may know better than to say, "Math is too hard for you," but the message still comes through. The talking Barbie doll who says, "Math is hard," is a glaring example of the battle that educators face in providing gender equity. Even though that model of Barbie doll was recalled from toy stores, teachers must undo continuing negative messages from other sources and replace them with positive ones. In some regards, girls are treated better than boys at school—and those practices need to be preserved for girls and extended to boys.

Teachers often complain that parental influence and peer influence are so strong that teachers can't make much of a difference. Yet students spend many hours in classrooms in which teachers dominate the interactions, rewards, and punishments. By the time a student enters junior high, she or he has typically spent more time with teachers than with a father and probably as much as with a mother. By this time, teachers have had about seven thousand hours with a student; surely that is enough time to make a difference. Teachers are the main people, outside of the immediate family, who define to students who they are, what kind of students they are, what they can expect from life, and how society will value them. Teachers define academic success and failure. Their expectations, demands, and attributions profoundly influence students. Teachers, more than parents or peers, control classroom achievement.

The research literature shows that teachers can and do change their behavior with good staff development and in-service programs. In fact, the most significant teacher variable associated with school success has been found to be the quality of teacher training.[37] You can reduce gender inequity, and you can make a difference.

ENDNOTES

1. Hesse, P., and Cross, S. (1990). "Star Wars or Rainbows as Defense against Evil? Messages about Conflict Resolution on Boys' and Girls' Television." International Society of Political Psychology, Thirteenth Annual Scientific Meeting, Washington, DC, July 11–14.

2. Condry, J., and Condry, S., (1976). "Sex Differences: A Study of the Eye of the Beholder." *Child Development, 47,* pp. 812–819. For similar studies, see also Seavey, C.A., et al. (1975), "Baby X: The Effect of Gender Labels on Adult Responses to Infants." *Sex Roles, 1,* pp. 103–109; and Will, J.A. et al. (1976). "Maternal Behavior and Perceived Sex of Infant." *American Journal of Orthopsychiatry, 46,* pp. 135–139.

3. Fagot, B. (1978). "The Influence of Sex of Child on Parental Reactions to Toddler Children." *Child Development, 49,* pp. 459–465.
4. Maccoby, E. and Jacklin, C. (1987) "Gender Segregation in Childhood." In H.W. Reese (ed.), *Advances in Child Development and Behavior, 20,* pp. 195–216. New York: Academic Press.
5. The following discussion is based on Maccoby, E. (1990). "Gender and Relationships: A Developmental Account." *American Psychologist, 45,* pp. 513–520.
6. Tannen, D. (1990). *You Just Don't Understand: Women and Men in Conversation.* New York: William Morrow and Co.
7. Tannen, D. (1990), pp. 44–45.
8. Maccoby, E. (1990), pp. 513–520.
9. Cherry, L. (1975). "The Preschool Teacher–Child Dyad: Sex Differences in Verbal Interaction." *Child Development, 46,* pp. 532–535.
10. Tannen, D. (1990), p. 255.
11. Honig, A.S., and Wittmer, D.S. (1982). "Teacher Questions to Male and Female Toddlers." *Early Child Development and Care, 9,* pp. 19–32.
12. The following discussion is based on Sadker, M., Sadker, D., and Klein, S. (1991), "The Issue of Gender in Elementary and Secondary Education," in G. Grant (ed.) *Review of Research in Education 17,* Washington, D.C.: American Educational Research Association.
13. Maccoby, E. (1990), pp. 513–520.
14. Lockheed, M. (1986). "Reshaping the Social Order: The Case of Gender Segregation." *Sex Roles, 14,* pp. 617–628.
15. Askew, S. and Ross, C. (1988). *Boys Don't Cry: Boys and Sexism in Education.* Philadelphia, PA: Open University Press.
16. LeBlanc, A.N. (September 1992). "Harassment in the Halls." *Seventeen,* pp. 163–165, 170.
17. Eagley, A.H. (1987). *Sex differences in social behavior: A social role interpretation.* Hillsdale, NJ: Erlbaum.
18. Van Velsor, E. and Hughes, M. (1990). *Gender Differences in the Development of Managers: How Women Managers Learn from Experience.* San Diego, CA: Center for Creative Leadership.
19. Conn, C. and Silverman, H. (1991). *What Counts,* p. 176. New York: Henry Holt and Co.
20. Conn, C. and Silverman, H. (1991), p. 178.
21. Conn, C. and Silverman, H. (1991), p. 177.
22. See Maria Matute-Bianchi's discussion of the heterogeneity of students of Mexican descent. Matute-Bianchi, M.E. (1991). "Situational Ethnicity and Patterns of School Performance among Immigrant and Nonimmigrant Mexican-Descent Students." In M. Gibson and J. Ogbu (eds.),

Minority Status and Schooling: A Comparative Study of Immigrant and Involuntary Minorities. New York: Garland Publishing Co.

23. Conn, C. and Silverman, H. (1991), p. 39.

24. This example is based on information in J. Ogbu's (1991) "Low School Performance as an Adaptation: The Case of Blacks in Stockton, California." In M. A. Gibson and J. U. Ogbu's (eds.) *Minority Status and Schooling.*

25. AAUW Report, p. 34.

26. Slavin, R. (1991). *Educational Psychology.* Englewood Cliffs, NJ: Prentice Hall.

27. Bem, S. (1975). "Sex Role Adaptability: One Consequence of Psychological Androgyny." *Journal of Consulting and Clinical Psychology, 31,* pp. 634–643.

28. Steinberg, L., Dornbusch, S.M., and Brown, B.B. (1990). "Ethnic Differences in Adolescent Achievement." *American Psychologist, 47,* pp. 723–729.

29. Brown, L. and Gilligan, C. (1992). *Meeting at the Crossroads: Women's Psychology and Girls' Development.* Cambridge, MA: Harvard University Press.

30. Fordham, S. and Ogbu, J. (1986). "Black Students' School Success: Coping with the Burden of 'Acting White.' " *Urban Review, 18,* pp. 176–206.

31. For more information on sex differences in adolescence, see a Spring 1987 (vol. 7) Special Issue of *Journal of Early Adolescence.*

32. Conn, C. and Silverman, H. (1991), p. 40.

33. Kelly, C. "The Miss America Syndrome," *Sassy Magazine,* April 1992, p. 63.

34. For a fuller discussion of this, see Belenky, M. et al. (1986). *Women's Way of Knowing,* New York: Basic Books; and Tannen, D. (1990), *You Just Don't Understand: Men and Women in Conversation,* New York: William Morrow and Co.

35. For a fuller discussion of learning and performance goals see Dweck, C. (1989) "Motivation." In A. Lesgold and R. Glaser (eds.), *Foundations for a Psychology of Education.* Hillsdale, NJ: Lawrence Erlbaum Associates.

36. Marianne LaFrance (1985) makes this and other interesting points in "The School of Hard Knocks: Nonverbal Sexism in the Classroom," *Theory into Practice, 24,* pp. 41–44.

37. Irvine, J.J. (1991). *Black Students and School Failure: Policies, Practices, and Prescriptions.* New York: Praeger.

3 Strategies for Achieving Gender Equity

The best way to achieve gender equity in the classroom is to improve classroom learning generally. In this chapter, we'll learn thirteen strategies to create a better learning environment. If you're already a teacher, you can begin immediately to use these strategies in your classroom. If you're studying to become a teacher, you'll want to look for ways these strategies could be used in the classrooms that you observe. Each will be discussed in depth:

1. Perform a gender-bias audit of the classroom.
2. Teach self-assessment.
3. Encourage risk-taking and help students to set goals.
4. Teach students to take pride in success, but to learn from mistakes.
5. Provide good feedback.
6. Avoid negative messages.
7. Retrain attributions.
8. Reduce stereotypical thinking.
9. Redirect selective attention.
10. Remember individual differences.
11. Use groups effectively.
12. Teach the "evaded curriculum."
13. Focus on math and science.

STRATEGY 1: PERFORM A GENDER BIAS
AUDIT OF THE CLASSROOM

Gender bias exists in most classrooms. As you go through this section, you will probably find out you're not as bias-free as you believe. Even great teachers and near-perfect parents sometimes treat boys and girls differently. Self-knowledge can be painful, but remember you have been socialized, like everyone else, to be part of a society that treats girls and boys very differently. So don't be too hard on yourself if you find significant room for improvement!

If you're teaching or student teaching, you'll focus on your own classroom. If you're preparing to teach, you'll focus on a classroom that you're observing. If the classroom isn't yours, share these materials with the teacher first. Be sure the teacher understands what you're doing and why. Go through the checklist and analyses to find the "hot spots" in the classroom and in your style or the style of the teacher whom you're observing. If you're the teacher, you can do the first part alone. Make notes as you go. For the second part, involving another teacher will help. You can't make changes unless you're aware of the problem. If you're doing this audit as an observer, you can do both parts by yourself.

This audit will be time consuming, but well worth your time. Unless you become aware of an inequity, you can't correct it. You probably believe good classrooms are free of any bias, but prepare to be surprised at the results. Let's start by using Gender Audit, Part I to look at the room itself.

GENDER AUDIT, PART I

☐ **Walls and bulletin boards**

  ☐ Are females and minority groups represented—and not just in stereotypical presentations?

_____

_____

_____

  ☐ Are females active participants and not just shown in the background?

_____

_____

_____

_____

  ☐ Are males shown in nurturing and helping roles?

_____

_____

_____

  ☐ Look at which students' work is displayed. Are girls and boys equally represented in all areas?

_____

_____

_____

_____

☐ **Consider next the supplementary materials.**

☐ If there are extra readings, do they depict women and girls in a wide range of activities? Are girls as well as boys involved in active play, showing initiative, solving problems, being independent, brave, and strong?

_____

_____

_____

_____

☐ Are boys and men shown in nonstereotyped ways? Are they shown being sensitive or tender?

_____

_____

_____

_____

☐ Are there books about nontraditional men and women?

_____

_____

_____

_____

☐ Be sure the books on the reading list and in the classroom show positive images of females.

☐ Consider films and other instructional media. Are women and girls fairly represented?

☐ Does the library have nonsexist resources?

☐ Does the library have separate sections labelled "Books for Boys" or "Books for Girls"? (If so, discourage them!)

☐ **Consider activities and extra-curricular programs**

    ☐ What activities are available at recess? Do girls and boys have access to the same activities and equipment?

_____

_____

_____

    ☐ Look at clubs and other extra-curricular activities. Are there comparable ones for boys and girls? Are most of them integrated? Are they highly sex-typed (e.g., Future Homemakers of America for girls and Science Club for boys)?

_____

_____

_____

    ☐ Look at formal courses. Are all courses open to both boys and girls? Are girls and boys encouraged to take nontraditional courses?

    ☐ Are fathers given special encouragement to attend PTA or to become involved?

    ☐ Is it assumed that mothers will be classroom volunteers or be the ones to bake cookies?

☐ **Classroom arrangement**

    ☐ Who sits where and why? Are boys and girls seated differently? If so, examine the rationale.

_____

_____

_____

☐ When students work in groups, how are the groups determined and why? Are there sex-segregated groups?

_____

_____

_____

☐ **Look across the room at random times throughout the day.**

   ☐ Who's where, doing what? Are the girls and boys in different places, doing different things?

_____

_____

_____

_____

_____

   ☐ Are boys doing more "doing" and girls doing more watching?

_____

_____

_____

_____

☐ **Look at graded assignments.**

   ☐ Were similar comments given for equivalent work?

_____

_____

   ☐ Did girls receive *excessive* praise in math or science, thereby sending a "low-ability" message?

_____

_____

☐ **Look especially at comments with regard to effort.**

   ☐ Were different assumptions made about how hard different students have worked?

_____

_____

_____

   ☐ Were different recommendations made for additional work?

_____

_____

_____

☐ Look at recommendations for improvement. Are they the same for boys and girls?

_____

_____

_____

_____

_____

☐ Look at criticism. Have boys received more than girls?

_____

_____

_____

_____

_____

☐ **Classroom management**

☐ Carefully examine the rules and methods. What are the biggest behavior problems? Are the problem behaviors more common among boys or girls? Do the rules apply in the same way for all students? Are punishment and rewards applied consistently? Which students seem to be in trouble more?

_____

_____

_____

_____

_____

☐ If you are the teacher, set a tape recorder going when the students are entering the room and when they are leaving. If you're an observer, listen to the teacher's casual conversations. Are different kinds of things said to boys and girls? Is the same amount of casual conversation directed to boys and girls?

_____

_____

_____

_____

_____

_____

_____

_____

_____

_____

_____

_____

☐ **Keep scoring sheets handy and record your responses to the following:**

  ☐ Keep track of requests for help from students and teacher responses. Do girls or boys ask for more help? Are responses to requests different?

Student Requests for Help

Girls	Boys

☐ Keep track of what kind of help is offered to students. Do boys and girls get different kinds of help? When boys are helped, do they get more constructive feedback?

Helping Behavior

Girls	Boys

☐ Keep track of when the teacher requests help from students or when students are assigned classroom tasks. Do girls and boys get asked for the same kinds of help? Are they assigned to the same types of tasks?

Teacher Requests for Help

Girls	Boys

☐ When a student has an emotional outburst, make a note of the teacher's response. After you've collected a dozen or so examples, see if there are differences in responses to girls versus boys.

Responses to Emotion

Girls	Boys

Look back at this chart and ask yourself the following questions:
☐ Did one group receive more sympathy?
☐ Did the teacher offer distractions for one group more than the other?
☐ Did the teacher address feelings more for one group than the other?
☐ Did the teacher take one group's concerns more seriously?

☐ Look at who gets punished or reprimanded, why and how. Are there differences between the girls and boys?

Punishment

Girls	Boys

For the next group of items, you'll use Gender Audit, Part II to look at very subtle behaviors, of which you are probably unaware. Ideally, you should videotape several representative segments of your class. Audio tape will work, too, and may be less intimidating to your students. Try to tape discussions of two different types, such as language arts and math. If possible, find a colleague who's also interested in doing this analysis on a class and score each other's tapes. The most objective scoring will result from scoring only one or two categories at a time, then rewatching the tape to score other dimensions.

GENDER AUDIT, PART II

☐ **Teacher style**

    ☐ Keep track of whom is asked questions, as well as the difficulty of the questions. Do boys get asked more difficult questions?

Questions

Girls	*Boys*

☐ In classroom discussions, what kind of hints or clues are given when a student doesn't immediately get the right answer?

Hints/Clues

Girls	Boys

☐ Keep track of what kind of praise students are given. Are there differences between boys and girls?

Praise

Girls	Boys

☐ Keep track of criticisms. Are girls and boys criticized differently? Look especially at constructive versus negative criticism.

Criticism

Girls	*Boys*

☐ Keep track of when students are interrupted. Who gets interrupted and who does the interrupting, a girl or a boy? Do you see any sex differences?

Interruptions

Girls Interrupted		Boys Interrupted	
By girls	*By boys*	*By girls*	*By boys*

☐ Keep track of exactly what is said after a student gives an answer. Is something neutral such as "mmm" or "okay" more likely to be said to girls and something positive, such as "Good point," to boys?

Responses to Students

Girls	Boys

☐ Teachers sometimes call on boys as a way of managing behavior. Because girls tend to be better behaved, teachers don't need to call on them as frequently as a way to keep them awake or attentive. Is this the pattern in this class?

Who Is Called On

Girls	Boys

☐ Teachers sometimes stand near boys or speak more directly to them as another way of managing behavior. Is this the pattern in this class?

Who the Teacher Stands Near

Girls	Boys

☐ Look also at student-initiated behaviors. Students who initiate more are likely to be judged more fairly. If a student doesn't initiate, the teacher usually relies on stereotype.

Positive student initiating behaviors include volunteering information, raising a hand to speak, beginning work independently, or seeking appropriate assistance. Negative initiating behaviors might include seeking attention through misbehavior, seeking inappropriate help, or in some other way violating a class rule.

Student-Initiated Behaviors

Girls		Boys	
Positive	Negative	Positive	Negative

Most teachers find that boys initiate more behaviors—both positive and negative—than do girls. If you're a teacher and this is the pattern you find, you'll want to focus on changing the students' behavior so that girls increase positive initiating behavior and boys reduce negative initiating behavior.

You probably found some differences between what girls and boys experience in the classroom. Like most people, you were unaware of the subtle ways in which you and others treat children differently. In order to change your behavior, you first have to bring it to consciousness. This exercise may have helped. If not, try visiting a group of infants and toddlers with whom you are unfamiliar. As you look around, make note of which children are male and which are female and how you made your determination. Most of the time, this will be done on the basis of clothes and hairstyles rather than on their behavior. There will be a group of children dressed in a more unisex fashion. You'll find it difficult, if not impossible, to determine their sex by simply observing their behavior.

Then focus on the toddlers' caregivers and see if you can identify the children's sex by the caregivers' *behavior.* Watch for differences in how they talk to the babies, how they handle them, how they try to comfort them, what toys they offer them. You might notice, for example, how caregivers react to a child's crying after the mother leaves. In some cases, they try to distract the child by offering a toy, teaching the child to ignore feelings. In another case, they might offer comfort, "Oh, you miss your momma. Don't worry, she'll be back. She loves you." In which case do you suppose the child is a boy and in which is a girl? When it's time for clean up, you'll notice some toddlers are urged to help and others aren't. Which do you suppose are the girls and which the boys? Listen for compliments. Do you suppose the "Oh, don't you look cute!" is more likely directed toward a girl or a boy? Listen for compliments on achievement. Do boys get more?

If you teach older children, ask them to monitor your behavior and to let you know when you treat girls and boys differently. Use the following checklist as a guide for observation.

Becoming more aware of your own behavior is the most important step towards gender equity in your classroom.

CHECKLIST

Do I:

☐ speak softly to girls and more harshly to boys?

☐ criticize boys more?

☐ criticize boys more publicly?

☐ praise girls and boys equally?

☐ assign different housekeeping chores to boys and girls?

☐ talk to girls more about feelings?

☐ let boys call out answers more than girls?

☐ ask specifically for a boy or a girl when I need a volunteer?

☐ allow all students equal access to equipment and materials?

☐ put girls and boys in separate groups for projects?

STRATEGY 2: TEACH SELF-ASSESSMENT

People in general are not very good at evaluating themselves. It's always hard to be objective, but to be objective about *yourself* is a real challenge. Yet knowing yourself, your strengths and weaknesses, allows you to set appropriate goals and plan effectively. Time management is impossible if you don't know how long a task will take you. Self-assessment is particularly important to students. They have to assess their work and decide when it's "good enough" to turn in or whether it needs revision. They have to decide when they've mastered a topic and can stop studying. They have to know when to ask for help, whom to ask, and what to ask. Self-assessment also affects expectations and satisfaction. Level of satisfaction usually depends more on expectations and self-assessment than actual performance.

Women and girls often have problems with self-assessment. They tend toward under-confidence, which is one reason they often set lower goals and avoid risks. There are a variety of reasons why self-assessment is particularly troublesome for them. For one, women and girls tend to be highly dependent on others' opinions and evaluations of their performance. To boys, performance is more likely to stand alone. They are more apt to say, "I did well," while girls are more apt to say, "*The teacher said* I did well." Because women and girls are less likely than men and boys to receive accurate and critical feedback, it's difficult for girls to learn to assess their own work. Because they tend to be more relationship-oriented, they naturally focus on others' perceptions.

Girls often over-study because they're anxious to please the teacher, do well, and make everyone happy. Girls often learn when their papers are ready to turn in and when they're ready for the exam by an external timetable: the paper's ready when it's due and it's time to stop studying just before the exam on exam day. Over-preparation works well in high school and even into college. But when girls grow up and the demands increase, they often have difficulty with time management because they feel the need to make everything perfect.

Boys tend to *under-prepare* for schoolwork. Under-preparation, however, gets corrected. A bad grade is the result, and the boy knows he needs to study more next time. But girls' *over*-preparation rarely gets corrected because a *good* grade usually results. To make matters worse, girls worry that the teacher will be disappointed if they don't perform well. Boys are typically less concerned with what the teacher thinks of them. For boys, this pattern often starts in early adolescence when they distance themselves from everything feminine as they try to establish their masculine identity. Most of their teachers are women, so they don't want to be like the teacher. Girls, however, want to be like the teacher and strive to accomplish that by having the teacher like them.

I once overheard my daughter expressing outrage that my son had decided not to do his homework. He patiently explained that he had an "A" aced, even with a zero on that night's assignment. Further, he knew the material and the teacher knew he knew it. So why bother? My daughter, indignant at the idea, exclaimed, "But it will hurt the teacher's feelings! She'll think you're lazy and don't care." He found that idea amusing, pointing out that if the teacher really cared, perhaps she ought to get a life. This exchange is fairly typical of the different way in which the sexes often look at tasks. To boys and men, a task is something that needs to get done. To girls and women, a task is more likely to have *significance*. A task may be symbolic of the whole relationship. That's why for some women, it's essential to bake a birthday cake rather than buy one—baking it yourself shows that you really care. To a father, a child's birthday party is probably just a child's birthday party. To a mother, however, it may be a symbol of her relationship with her child as well as a symbol of her value as a mother. Under the latter interpretation, having everything perfect is obviously much more important! This difference in attitude goes back to the attributional styles we discussed earlier. Women and girls are more likely to believe a poor showing is part of a general pattern that reflects stable and personal characteristics that are predictive of the future. Failure is direct evidence that they are not worthy.

Better self-assessment is one way to get around dysfunctional attributions. Clearly understanding your own role in success and failure and having realistic expectations will lead to correctly labeling the internal and external factors that led to your performance. You'll know whether the low grade was because you didn't study enough or because the test was harder than usual or because the teacher was unfair. Girls and women who can evaluate their own work are hindered less by a society that gives them ineffective feedback and sometimes discriminates against them. Being able to assess your own work frees you from dependence on others. Luckily, self-assessment can be taught, and we turn now to some simple, straightforward strategies for teachers to enhance their students' ability to evaluate their own work.

To teach self-assessment, *ask students to predict how they will perform* on an upcoming task. Just making predictions forces students to think about and evaluate their performance. It focuses their attention on task demands and their level of preparation. Many students see grades simply as something the teacher does to them with no rhyme or reason. Ask about the basis for their prediction. Then talk about why their prediction was proven accurate or inaccurate by their actual performance. Some examples follow.

Teacher: You have a test coming up tomorrow. What grade do you expect to make?
Student 1: I think I can make a B.

Teacher: What makes you think so?

Student 1: Well, I usually do pretty well in math, and this material isn't any harder than usual. I've turned in all my homework and I did well on the pop quiz yesterday. I'm going to study extra hard tonight.

After the test:

Teacher: What was your prediction?

Student 1: I thought I'd make a B, but I made an A!

Teacher: Why were you wrong?

Student 1: I guess I was worried about finishing on time. I thought I might have to hurry and might make some careless errors.

Teacher: But you didn't! I remember your last test—you didn't have time for the last problem and you made several arithmetic errors. Why did you do better this time?

Student 1: I think maybe the drills we did in class helped me. I got faster after that. Maybe I should practice like that on my own some.

Teacher: Good idea. I have some workbooks with extra problems if you want to borrow them.

Or another scenario:

Teacher: We've got a test coming up. How do you think you'll do?

Student 2: I dunno. I can never predict. Guess it depends on your mood.

Teacher: Well, let's think about it. How have you done so far?

Student 2: Not so hot. I failed a couple of tests.

Teacher: Let's look at your grades. You got a C on the third test. Why do you think you did better on that one?

Student 2: I dunno. Guess it was easy.

Teacher: It was over adding fractions. Do you remember?

Student 2: Yeah, that made more sense to me.

Teacher: I see, too, that you turned in all your homework that week. Also you didn't miss any classes. Do you think that might have helped?

Student 2: Yeah, I guess so.

Teacher: Let's talk about the two times that you made an F. One was right before spring break. Do you remember what was going on then?

Student 2: Oh, yeah. My mom was sick and didn't remind me to do my homework.

Teacher: Maybe you should work on doing it without being reminded. You can see that it helps your grade. You've done a good job on this unit—your homework has been pretty good. Do you feel like you understand what we've been doing?

Student 2: I dunno.

Teacher: Maybe a practice test would help you figure out how prepared you are?

After the practice test:

Teacher: You got 75 percent right. What do you think?
Student 2: I dunno.
Teacher: Well, let's look at each section. You did well on the first part, subtracting fractions. But your errors mostly were on the last part, on multiplying fractions.
Student 2: Yeah, that's really hard. Maybe I need to work more on that.
Teacher: Good idea. Sue could help you.

Later:

Teacher: How did it go with Sue?
Student 2: Okay, I guess. I think I understand it now. We worked some problems and I got most of them right.
Teacher: Good! Now, what do you think you'll make on tomorrow's exam?
Student 2: Well, it seems I should be able to get a C if the problems are like the ones in the book.
Teacher: They will be.
Student 2: Will we have the whole period?
Teacher: Yeah.
Student 2: Then, I shouldn't be too hurried. If I go slow and doublecheck my work that helps.
Teacher: Good idea.

After the test:

Teacher: How was your prediction?
Student 2: Right on target!
Teacher: Great! Once you pinpoint your problem, it's easier to do something about it.

Predictions don't have to be made one-on-one with the students. Teachers can ask the whole class to write down their predictions, and after the test, ask them to think about the accuracy of their predictions. Simply focusing on predictions focuses attention on self-assessment.

Have students evaluate their own work. Ask students to grade their own paper. Afterwards, you grade it and compare the differences. What did you criticize that they overlooked? Talk with them about discrepancies between your own evaluation and theirs. *Having clear grading guidelines is another way to help students evaluate their own work.* They can only evaluate their own work in a way that corresponds to your grade if the standards are clear. Talk to students about how you grade and why. Never simply give a grade; explain what makes it an A or a C paper.

Peer review is another way to help students see how standards apply and to become more focused on evaluation. Peer review forces students to take the perspective of the audience, which then helps them see their own work from the audience's perspective. Often students are defensive and resistant to criticisms made by the teacher. When other students make similar comments, it's much more likely to have an effect. Peer review is also a way to provide students with extra feedback. One reality of teaching is that teachers lack the time to give each student extensive feedback on each piece of work. In peer review, the students do not grade each other's work; they critique it. Peer reviewers react to the clarity and the quality of arguments. If you use peer review, it's a good idea to have carefully prepared instructions. A good starting place is to ask reviewers to indicate the good points as well as the weak points.[1]

Teach students to reward themselves for a job well done. Just as you may reward yourself after grading ten papers by watching a television program, students can learn to evaluate and monitor their own performance, and then provide their own reward. Something as simple as teaching students to say to themselves "Good job!" can help. This is especially important for girls because they may not get the same level of rewards as boys. Looking back at the class of 1972 NLS data, women clearly were not getting the same kind of financial rewards as men. We can only hope that there were some intrinsic rewards available to them. Self-reward is a powerful motivational tool.

Ask for predictions on many things. "What do you think the score will be for Saturday's game?" "How long will it take you to read that chapter?" "How many laps can you run?" "How many snow days do you think we'll have this year?" In cases like the latter, you can look at data from previous years or see how many snow days the school has had so far. Then discuss the basis for different predictions. Making predictions and seeing if you're right is fun and focuses students on evaluating all aspects of a situation. It teaches students to analyze data.

Get students to make predictions based on larger sets of data. People have a tendency to base predictions on immediate or highly salient events. For example in sports, rather than focusing on only the last game, refocus attention on the whole season. When predicting grades, have students consider all of a semester's work rather than one extremely good or extremely poor grade or their last grade. When students focus on a mistake, remind them of the bigger picture—the many things that they did correctly. It's especially important to put a failure in a larger context so that it will be perceived as an unusual event rather than the norm. If a student consistently fails, the teacher must find some way for the student to experience *genuine success*. In that way, the teacher can discuss a failing grade in the context of other, acceptable work. (More on this later.)

Model self-assessment. "I'm starting an exercise class tonight. I think I can do fifteen push-ups because I am in good shape." Then, the next day, "I was wrong about those fifteen push-ups! I could only do ten. I didn't take into account how strong your arms have to be. I'm in good shape over all, but my arms are not very strong." *Or* "I think I can have your exams graded by Thursday because there are twenty-five of them and it takes me about fifteen minutes to grade each one. I won't be able to grade any on Wednesday, but I'll have time on Monday and Tuesday." *Or* "I think we can work through page ninety-two by the end of next week if we do two pages every day in class and two for homework. But the next unit is harder, so we can't expect to move quite as fast."

When most people assess themselves, they do it on the basis of general ability. They say, "I'm good in math; therefore I'll do well on this math test." You want to push your students a little further. Teach them to think in specifics: Is this material easier or harder than usual? Have you studied more or less than usual? Will the format or time make it easier or more difficult for you? Is there anything different from usual that might affect your performance (a cold, extra work in other classes, more time on extracurricular activities, more duties at home)?

Reward self-assessment. Talk about the value of self-knowledge with your students. Praise students who are able to evaluate their own work accurately. Show self-assessment as a valuable skill. Ask students, "Now that you know where you are, how can you use that knowledge to do even better?" Help them to use their self-evaluation to develop their skills and to make plans.

Rewarding self-assessment is more difficult than you might think. Most teachers send the message that "more is better." They tend to reward the obsessive student who over-studies and does much more than is required (usually a girl). But working with students to prioritize tasks and to allot time accordingly is much more beneficial. Students need to learn to study for the exam until they have mastered the material, not until time for the test. Time management is one of the most important job skills, yet it is virtually impossible to manage time effectively unless you have good self-assessment skills.

Use the following Exhibit to study some examples of how teachers can focus on self-assessment and prediction in everyday situations.

EXHIBIT

Example	Teacher Response
Paula made a 1400 on her SATs and was 100 percent certain she would get accepted to Duke.	When she didn't get in, we talked about her expectation. She believed that since the average score there was 1300, she should have gotten in. We then talked about all the other factors that go into the decision and evaluated her with regard to those other factors.
Henry lost his temper and handled a situation poorly. He now feels bad and says he can't be a good student leader.	I pointed out how unusual this was for him and that he has a record of successes as a leader. We talked about what he could learn from his error and how it wasn't nearly as bad as his perception made it. I reassured him that all leaders occasionally fail to reach their expectations.
Sylvia made a 100 on her spelling test and is overconfident about her upcoming semester test. She says she won't have to study much.	I reminded her that the 100 was the result of more study and drill than usual. I showed her some earlier, lower grades and urged her to make a list of words she missed on earlier tests and plan how to study efficiently for the big test.
Sally tends to be overly anxious and tense about her work. This week she handed in an excellent paper early and remarked, "I wanted to leave myself free this weekend."	I said, "Good idea. You did an excellent job and there's no need to obsess over it any longer."
Jahan explained that he spent the week working hard on his college admissions forms and apologized for what was for him a sloppy homework assignment. He saw that he had not managed his time well and promised to do better next time.	I said, "Yes, having something extra to do can cut into your homework time. I'm glad you're learning about time management now."

(continued)

Example	Teacher Response
Manda predicted she'd make an A on her math test, but made a D.	We went over her test and reviewed her homework that corresponded to each part of the test. I explained that she missed the same kinds of problems on the test that she'd missed on her homework. I had her reconsider how well she understood the material. Then we developed a plan to learn what she had misunderstood.
Lamont had predicted he would fail the test, but actually made a C. When asked, he explained that the teacher had "given" him the grade and that he didn't really deserve it.	I showed him the grading key and went through his exam to convince him that he'd earned every point. We talked about the basis for his prediction and it seemed to be based on his general lack of self-confidence rather than an analysis of his readiness for this particular exam.

Some activities are especially good for developing good self-assessment skills. Chess is one of them.[2] Tournament chess gives students constant feedback about their performance in the form of skill ratings. The link between performance and ratings is direct, clearly observable, and public. Every game has a loser, so students learn it's okay to fail and how to learn from their failures. Even though losing is common, success—in terms of accelerating ratings—is the norm. Any student who works at it will find his or her rating goes up. In one study of players in the ninth grade and below, players with higher ratings were more accurate than lower-rated players in their predictions of how they'd do in future games.[3] But they were not more confident. In fact, the worse the student's rating, the more he or she overestimated chances of winning! This shows that being able to judge your own skills and abilities is more important than simply having high hopes. Self-confidence is a fine thing, but *deserved self-confidence* is better.

Teachers are frequently urged to build students' self-confidence by telling them, "You can do anything you want to do." I think teachers should instead help students evaluate where they are, set realistic goals, and develop plans to reach them. Yes, you can do anything you want to do *if* you identify and develop the requisite skills and put in the necessary effort. Knowing where you're going and how you're going to get there makes a student feel in control and that builds deserved self-confidence. Students who can set realistic goals experience success, and they know that success is due to their own efforts. This builds deserved self-confidence rather than cockiness. Students are notoriously unrealistic about success. Many expect to take easy courses, make mediocre grades, and then get great jobs making lots of money, but without having to work too hard. Teachers can do students a great service by providing a little reality check! Students need to learn to monitor and realistically assess their skills and performance. Only then can they control their own learning.

When a teacher can answer the questions in the Exhibit, she or he has been successful teaching self-assessment. If you can answer them all about a class you're teaching, reward yourself!

EXHIBIT

QUESTIONS TO ASK YOURSELF

1. What are my students' expectations that their efforts will lead to successful performance?

2. Are the students over-confident or under-confident?

3. Can they make sound predictions of performance on specific tasks? Or, do they operate on the basis of a global self-assessment (e.g., "I'm a lousy student")?

4. Do my students have adequate self-management skills? Do they know how to plan, how to study, how to find help and resources, how to manage their time, and how to set goals?

5. Do my students have an accurate idea of the amount of effort that is necessary for successful performance on each task? Do they adjust their effort on the basis of task difficulty, feedback, and so forth?

6. Can students accurately evaluate their own performance? Do they use feedback to adjust their evaluations?

7. Can my students use self-rewards?

8. Are my students deservedly self-confident?

STRATEGY 3: ENCOURAGE RISK-TAKING AND HELP STUDENTS SET GOALS

Goal setting is closely related to self-assessment. What people think they can do, rather than what they can actually do, determines their choice of goals. Students who can evaluate their work will benefit more from goal setting than those students who rely solely on the teacher's evaluation.

Goal setting is motivating because it focuses attention on the goal. When students accept ownership of a goal, they are more likely to reach it. Goal setting enhances self-evaluation and self-esteem because students can chart their progress relative to the goal, rather than relative to other students. Individual goal setting is a good way to accommodate differences in student ability. Monitoring their own progress also places students in a position of control because reaching their goal becomes their responsibility, not the teacher's. Students at all levels can help set their own goals. One popular way to do this is through contracts. Younger students in particular love legalistic-sounding contracts requiring signatures and seals.

We've talked earlier about the benefits of learning goals and the fact that girls tend to focus on them less than boys do. *Focus on learning goals whenever you can.* Performance goals usually depend on extrinsic rewards while learning goals depend on intrinsic rewards. Students who have learned to reward themselves are on the way to being motivated by intrinsic rewards. Teachers have to use extrinsic rewards some of the time with many students, but teachers should always be looking ahead as to how to develop students' intrinsic motivation. Focusing on learning goals is one way to do that.

How can teachers encourage learning goals? De-emphasizing grades and competitiveness is one way. In hopes of motivating students, teachers often place too much value on grades and standardized test scores. Grades are important, but they're supposed to be *measures* of learning, not an end in themselves. Remind students that the learning is more important. And remind them that if they take care of the learning, the performance will be just fine. Many students (and teachers) seem to have it backward: they see the learning as secondary to the grade.

Have you seen students who haggle over one half of a point on a test? Have you seen students who don't care about the content of what they learn, only what their grade is? Have you seen students take an easy rather than a challenging course so that they can maintain a perfect 4.0? These all result from too much emphasis on performance goals and not enough emphasis on learning goals. When my son was in the second grade, he once appeared by my bed at three A.M. to tell me he couldn't sleep because he was worried about tomorrow's achievement test! The teacher had told him he wouldn't be able to get into a good college if he didn't do well. Nobody—especially not a seven-year-old—needs that kind of pressure. Even the SAT people will let you take the test over.

Teachers can help by focusing on what students have learned and how the new knowledge or skill is benefiting them. *Focus on what students have learned rather than what they haven't learned.* Teachers can focus on improvement and even have improvement factored into grades. Learning goals can be rewarded in ways other than grades: *Find alternative ways to recognize learning.* Think of special recognition and awards for learning goals. At an end-of-the-year awards ceremony one year, I sat through endless awards for top grade in this and that. After seeing the same four or five students get awards over and over, one science teacher gave an award for the student who had asked the toughest questions. He accompanied the award with a nice speech about how asking questions was the essence of science and how there was one student (a girl) who had made him think all year by asking good questions.[4] With creativity, you can come up with interesting ways to let students know that learning is more important than grades.

Mastery learning techniques are especially good for learning goals. In mastery learning, the point is to master the material; the question of who finishes first is de-emphasized. Having opportunities for students to correct mistakes or do second drafts is another way to focus attention on learning goals. Time controls on tests often foster performance goals and unnecessary competitiveness. Ask yourself whether the appropriate goal is to be able to do one hundred math problems in fifteen minutes or to be able to correctly work all the problems in twenty-five minutes.

Students need to be persuaded that learning counts rather than grades. Every book on selective college admissions and every brochure from selective colleges stresses the importance of taking the most challenging coursework available and that a B in an Advanced Placement course is more highly valued than an A in Basket Weaving. Yet high school students continue to choose courses in terms of how it will affect their GPA. One ironic aspect of this is that the tougher courses improve standardized test scores, so that even if the GPA slips a bit, a higher SAT or ACT will compensate. You might show students these excerpts from two letters of recommendation and ask them to predict which student is more likely to obtain the scholarship. Tom's slightly higher GPA is not really that much of an advantage!

The following are some other characteristics of effective goals:

- Goals set by students themselves.

- Intermediate goals linked to long-term goals.

- Clearly stated goals with the means to reaching them clearly spelled out.

- Challenging goals (a student should be approximately 75 percent confident of reaching them).

- Goals with rewards attached to attaining them.

EXHIBIT

Dear Admissions Committee:

Tom is an excellent student and has a perfect 4.0 grade average. He is #1 in his class of ninety students. He studies hard and is always well prepared for exams. Although not my most original or creative student, he is conscientious and very hard working.

Dear Admissions Committee:

Tim is full of ideas and eager to learn. He enhanced our class discussions with information gathered through independent readings. In all my years of teaching, Tim has been one of the most exciting students I've had. His grades are very good—3.75 and he will graduate in the top 10 percent of his class.

Goals need to be challenging, which means there must be some risk attached. As we've learned, girls tend to avoid risk. There's nothing wrong with a little caution, but 75 percent success on challenging goals will get you farther than 100 percent success on trivial goals. One reason some people avoid risk is the high level of competitiveness in our society. When only a very few people "make it," people are understandably reluctant to make an error. The school years, however, should be a time of exploration when students can try out interests and ideas without heavy penalties for mistakes. There are a number of things teachers can do to encourage risk-taking. One is to *reduce the costs of failure.* Being able to drop a lowest grade or re-do a paper allows students the chance to experiment. Reward creativity even if it doesn't always lead to success. Avoid early evaluation. Have you ever worked in a group and offered an idea that was not quite worked out? Probably someone immediately pointed out all the problems and prevented the idea from developing. Don't be a nay-sayer. Watch a creative idea progress, offer suggestions and feedback along the way, but avoid premature criticism. Give students a chance to work through their ideas. Students often learn more from their failed attempts than from "safe" successes. Remind students that success typically comes after many failed attempts. The cleaning product "409" was named because it was the 409th attempt—the other 408 failed.

Teachers also need to talk with students about success. From watching television and listening to some teachers, students get the idea that success is something only a few persons achieve and that it's defined by having a high-status job and a lot of money. Some parents tell their children that they will be successful only if they become a physician or pursue some other high-status career. It's as though we took a normal curve, representing everyone, and told students, "You're only okay if you're in the top 10 percent." If only the best are good enough, then the other 90 percent of us aren't okay. The level of competition in our society has an especially harsh impact on girls and women. Some young girls believe that to be successful they have to make $200,000 per year, raise perfect children, and be a gourmet cook. I once read a profile on a female professor at Stanford, who had five children, played in the San Francisco symphony, had trekked across India by herself, was a marathon runner and a gourmet cook. She was also a world renowned-scholar. She's an ordinary role model!?

The message that only the top students are okay is particularly unfair to the rest of the students. While it's good to recognize the successes of the super-achievers, it's essential to find appropriate goals for *all* students and celebrate their attainment. Teachers have to redefine success so that it is available to all students. That means some goals should be noncompetitive and individualized. Students should be encouraged to compete against themselves and not just against each other.

As students enter their teen years, it becomes especially important to begin serious talks about the responsibilities of parenthood and how it might have an impact on career choices. Marriage today is often a partnership of equals, with both spouses following serious careers. Students who are beginning to plan for their futures need to be aware of the realities of dual responsibilities.

Go over your students' goals with them, helping them to find ways to achieve them and ways to monitor their progress. Charts and graphs are always a good idea. Set definite timetables. If the goals are unrealistic, help the students with self-evaluation or suggest an intermediate goal. Identify the rewards that will come with attainment. Check to see if any of the goals show evidence of gender bias. Do the girls set different types of goals? Talk to them and urge them to set goals that are truly challenging.

Teachers as well as students benefit from goals. One of your goals should be to reduce gender inequity in your classroom. Look back at the list of characteristics of effective goals for students and apply these characteristics to your goal of reducing gender inequity.

■ Goals that I have set myself.

Under which conditions would you enjoy working toward a goal of gender equity: (1) you're told you must or else lose your job or (2) you believe this goal is important and are deeply committed to it. Obviously, if reducing gender inequity is your own goal, you are more likely to be successful.

■ Intermediate goals linked to long-term goals.

Rather than simply stating the goal, can you think of intermediate goals? For example, an intermediate goal might be to do a gender audit of your classroom. Can you think of others? Write them below.

_____

_____

_____

_____

■ Clearly stated goals with the means to reaching them clearly spelled out.

The goal of reducing gender inequity is both broad and vague. Can you think what it might mean in your classroom? You might want to restate it in terms of subgoals. If you teach high school biology, for example, you may want to set a goal of having more girls from your class go on to take more science courses or have more girls participate in the school science fair. If you teach in the elementary grades, one of your goals might be to improve your interaction patterns so that you give equal time to both girls and boys. You'll need an action plan (the means to achieve your goal) to guide you in reaching your goal. Think in terms of how your short-term, intermediate goals, relate to your long-term goals. What outcomes do you anticipate from your actions? Try jotting down some initial ideas on the next Exhibit or try making your own chart. You'll be able to add to it as you work through this book.

■ Challenging goals (approximately 75 percent confident of reaching them).

Realistically, you are not going to re-do all of your lesson plans and completely change your interaction style next semester. Realistically, you are not going to persuade every girl in your biology class to take chemistry. Realistically, you are not likely to triple the number of girls who participate in the school science fair by next year. Your goals should be challenging, but not impossible.

■ Goals with rewards attached to attaining them.

Your rewards for reaching these goals will be mostly intrinsic. You probably won't get thanks from parents or more money from your principal, but you should see results that will make you proud. Be sure to notice and pat yourself on the back when they happen. When you do get discouraged, remember back to those "peak moments." Share your successes with others to encourage them, but also to ensure that you will gain support and encouragement for yourself. Be realistic about the rewards you can expect. You won't be able to change the world overnight!

EXHIBIT

ACTION PLAN TO ACHIEVE GENDER EQUITY IN MY CLASSROOM

Long-Term	Next Semester	Expected Outcomes
Changes/additions that I will make in materials.		
Changes that I will make in the way the course is organized/graded.		
Ways in which I will encourage goal setting.		
Changes that I will make in the way in which I interact with students.		
Ways in which I will encourage self-assessment by students.		

STRATEGY 4: TEACH STUDENTS TO TAKE PRIDE IN SUCCESS, BUT TO LEARN FROM MISTAKES

Students need some success. Repeated failure leads to learned helplessness.[5] But students don't need success all the time. In some forms of programmed learning, the steps are so tiny that many students whip through the programs with no errors. Sounds great. But what happens when a problem is difficult to solve? Students who've never experienced failure quit trying. In fact, this is just what happens in algebra classes all over the nation. Good students, for whom everything's been easy, suddenly get stuck and *very* frustrated. This is the very point at which many girls give up on math. They give up, not because they don't want to learn math, but because they expect to fail. As we've learned, girls are less likely to persist on difficult tasks. If we want students to persist in the face of repeated failure, we have to train them to deal with and learn from failure. Yet many teachers and parents work hard to protect students from failure—a big mistake. Students need to be taught to deal with failure. Girls in particular fear failure because for many girls, being a good student and making the teacher happy is the source of the bulk of their rewards in school. Who will like them if they make a mistake or fail?

Several things need to be done to make failing a worthwhile enterprise. First, teachers have to be sure it happens to everybody some of the time, but to nobody all of the time. If a student can't be academically successful at least some of the time, he or she is in the wrong place or the place is all wrong. No student should be placed in an environment where success is impossible. That means either moving the student or drastically changing the environment. Similarly if a student is successful *all* of the time, she or he is also in the wrong place or the place is all wrong. Every student deserves to be challenged. It's up to the school and the teacher to provide some challenge.

Unfortunately, many classrooms are environments in which some students fail all the time and some succeed all the time. Teachers who find themselves in this situation need guidance from school psychologists to place such students in appropriate environments. If you're lucky enough to have an extremely bright student who makes nothing but perfect grades, you need to work hard at challenging this student. You also have to let the student know that there will be times in the future when he or she will fail. When an all-A student brings home another perfect report card, most parents and teachers heap praise on the student, which sends the message that to be appreciated, the student needs to continue to be perfect. A better response would be, "You've done a good job again, but it looks to me like you're not being sufficiently challenged. Let's see if we can find some tougher courses for you. I don't want you to be bored. School will be more fun for you if it's challenging." Then when the student brings home the first "B," what should you say? I'd suggest, "Good, you've finally been challenged. I'm proud of you for working hard even when things weren't easy. You must be proud, too. I'd rather see you learn things and get a B than get A's and not learn as much."

Students can only learn from failure if they have plenty of success. It sounds ironic, but it's true. The "high" of success sustains students through the "low" of failure. So the first step to teaching students to learn from their failure is: *Find ways to provide success to all.* This must be legitimate, credible success. It's up to the teacher to find tasks on which the student has a good chance of succeeding and to teach the prerequisite skills. (They don't all have to be academic.) If a student consistently fails, it means he or she has been given inappropriate assignments or hasn't been taught the skills necessary to do them. On occasion, a student may have the skills, but be so demotivated that failure is inevitable. In that case, a teacher must find a way to motivate the student long enough to be successful, so that the student learns that hard work can lead to success. After the success, the teacher must be sure the student appreciates that her or his own hard work was responsible for the success and that future success is likely.

What do I mean by "legitimate" success? If a high school student brings in a cup of dirt for a science project and you award her a blue ribbon, this is not legitimate success. Students compare their efforts and rewards with other students and by middle elementary school, it's difficult to fool them. Preschoolers can each be told that their drawing is the best and they will each believe it. By middle elementary school, however, students have begun to compare their work and themselves to others and will not fall for fake praise. Providing excessive praise for what is obviously mediocre performance only lets the student know that you don't expect much from her. In the case of the cup of dirt science project, this student might have produced a legitimate project if she had worked in a cooperative group or under your close supervision. It's up to the teacher to structure assignments so that success is possible.

Not only must each student have a chance to succeed, each student must have a chance to make mistakes. Mistakes and failure are a part of everyone's life and all successful people have failed. Deborah Stipek reports that in Chinese schools, exams always have a few easy problems that everyone can solve and a few extremely difficult ones that no one can solve.[6] This teaches the class that no one succeeds all the time and that there's no shame in missing a problem. In the typical American classroom, in contrast, we have a caste system: those who always make 100's are at the top and those who always fail stay at the bottom. So another important step is to *provide failure opportunities for all students.* This means that all children must be challenged and "challenge" means occasional failure. When some educators talk about "challenging" students, they never mention failure! But that's doublespeak. Students can't be challenged without their making occasional serious mistakes.

Occasional failure is good therapy. We all have heard of excellent students who commit suicide because of a tiny perceived failure. We all know good students who during their first year in college are unable to deal with their first B or C grades. Surviving and learning from failure teaches students how to survive and learn from failure. Always succeeding leaves students without the tools to cope when failure occurs. Learning to persist in tough situations with many setbacks requires experience in just those kinds of situations. Yet teachers often provide little tasks with only slightly increasing difficulty in an effort to maximize success. But maximizing success is not the solution—*balancing* success and failure is better. Each student needs some of both.

Making sure that everyone struggles some of the time is also good for peer relations. Those students in the middle-ability and low-ability range need to see the top students working hard and struggling, too. Low-ability students often reject school values out of defensiveness. It's damaging to their egos to struggle when others obviously don't have to try hard to succeed. There's less to be defensive about when everyone struggles. All this struggling sounds depressing, and it can be if you don't *remind students of their successes.* By doing this, you are also teaching them to use their past experiences to motivate them through struggles. Self-talk is a critical motivational tool. Teach students to talk their way through tough tasks, reminding themselves that they've been successful in similar situations, to have patience, stay calm, and so forth.

One behavior that often gets in the way is *rumination.* This is when someone can't stop thinking about a failure and the mental "tape" keeps playing in their head, over and over. Women and girls tend to ruminate over failures more than do men and boys. This is probably because women and girls personalize, or attach more significance to their failures, seeing them as general indicators of ability and personal worth. You may be a ruminator. Do you dwell on a mistake so that you can't think about anything else? Rumination prevents you from focusing on strategies that will lead to success on the immediate problem. Remind yourself of the past only if you were successful. If you failed in the past, learn from it, then forget it. Good advice, but how do you stop rumination? Behavioral techniques work well. Some people put a rubberband around their wrist and every time the "bad thoughts" recur, they snap the rubberband and think to themselves, "No!" Another useful technique is to schedule a time to ruminate and then be done with it. Having a "good" memory ready to substitute for the "bad" memory can also work. In the dialogues below, a teacher helps students stop ruminating.

Student 1: Ever since I blew that play in last week's game, I haven't been able to concentrate. I blame myself. I keep replaying it over and over in my head. If I'd only listened to what the coach said, I wouldn't have made the mistake. Now every time I get the ball, I clutch.

Teacher: It's good to analyze what went wrong, but you're going overboard. Let's sit down after school and really analyze it to death. We'll learn everything there is to learn from the mistake. Write it all down in a long list. When you're satisfied that there's no more point in thinking about it, we'll have a symbolic ripping up of the list. Then when the thoughts creep back, you just remind yourself, there's nothing more to think about, the list is torn up and gone. If the thoughts still come back, wear this rubberband and snap it hard to remind yourself not to think about it. It sounds silly, but it works. You can control your thoughts if you work at it.

Student 2: Every time I sit down to take an exam, I keep thinking about that first test this semester. I just froze. I couldn't remember anything. I just stared and stared at the blank page. I'm afraid the same thing will happen again.

Teacher: I know how that can happen! I failed my driving test the first time I tried—I turned the wrong way down a one-way street. The next time I tried, I kept seeing the tester's face and hearing her yell. I got so nervous I ran a stop sign.

Student: Yeah, that's just what I mean.

Teacher: Why don't you plan tonight after dinner to sit for a half an hour and relive your test experience, think of everything you can about it. Maybe write down all your thoughts and fears, all the reasons why you froze. Tell yourself that's your time to think about it. In the meantime, if you start to think about it, tell yourself to wait till your scheduled time. Tomorrow if the thoughts come back, remind yourself that you already covered it. Also, have in mind that third test. Remember how well you did. If the "bad" test comes into mind, replace it with the "good" test. Go over the good test experience so that you can have a vivid image of exactly how you felt.

One way to learn from failure is to *perform a post-mortem after failure.* Sit down and really analyze what went wrong and plan for the future. Good chess players use the post-mortem strategy. The loser goes over the game in detail with the winner or a coach. The winner will identify errors, describe her strategy, and suggest alternative moves. They will replay the game with alternative moves to see how it might have turned out. Often the loser will learn that he almost won or that a winning strategy was at least possible. Listening to a chess player's post mortem is a fascinating way to see the value of failure. Losers come away feeling good because they learn that they had the winner really worried or that they came very close to beating a better player. Rather than a situation with two outcomes— winning or losing—the players appreciate the strengths and weaknesses of their various moves and their strategies. I've heard young players bragging that they had the state elementary champion worried or that they made a terrific move in a lost game. Isn't that better than feeling like a loser? They see the strengths of their losing game and the weaknesses of the winner's game. They also learn in very specific terms how to avoid future failure.

From observing hundreds of scholastic chess players over the years, I find it is possible to predict which players' chess ratings will go up by watching their post-game strategy. The players who sulk, fold up their boards, and go home are the ones whose ratings stagnate. Those who review their lost games are the ones whose ratings steadily climb. It's easy to analyze chess games because it's part of the chess culture—all good players do it. But in real life and in school, most of us are embarrassed by failure and work hard to hide it. We don't want to go over our mistakes, especially with peers or the teachers. Instead, we ruminate over them alone in the middle of the night.

The reason that we're embarrassed or humiliated by failure is that we've given failure a bad name. *Teachers need to redefine failure.* Failure needs to be seen as an opportunity for growth, a chance to diagnose what needs to be learned next. It's a necessary stage that one goes through before succeeding. It's something that everyone experiences and something that offers the best learning opportunity. Think about it: what's to learn from success? Success is good as a motivator, an uplifting experience that is self-validating. Success makes you feel good and we all need that. But if you really want to improve your skills, you need to know your limits and failure tells you what they are. Failure defines your next step. Success simply tells you that you reached the last step. Failure should focus you on the future and what needs to be done.

Too often, schoolwork has only two outcomes: the student succeeds or fails. For "A students," there's an A and anything else is failure. For other students, there's passing (a grade of D) or failing. Students need to be reminded that performance is a continuum. They can make a lot of mistakes, fail a lot of things, but that doesn't make them into a "loser." Winners don't succeed all the time, but they do *learn* all the time.

How can teachers convey failure as a good thing? First, by talking about failure in positive way. Failure shouldn't be a dirty word. Second, by modeling appropriate "failure talk." Teachers need to talk about their own mistakes and failures as learning experiences. Third, teachers need to create a climate in which failure and mistakes are accepted and don't define a student as a "loser." This climate should be one in which students are comfortable examining and analyzing failure situations—one in which analyzing failure is the norm. Fourth, teachers need to use failure in a positive rather than in a punishing way. Obviously, focusing on learning rather than on performance goals will help. Having opportunities to re-take tests, re-do papers, writing papers in drafts, and holding practice tests also helps. Avoid having the whole semester's grade depend on only one or two major exams.

Another useful technique is to *provide feedback without evaluation.* Most of us learn to dread feedback because it's usually associated with a negative evaluation. Criticize student work without assigning it a grade. Assignments should include some ungraded, but carefully read, work. This teaches students to separate the analysis of mistakes from their grade. Particularly in high school and college, grades are a necessary evil. Grades need to reflect differences among students' performance and this cannot be avoided. But students should learn the value of feedback without it engendering fear of failure.

STRATEGY 5: PROVIDE GOOD FEEDBACK

People learn from feedback, but not all feedback is "created equal." Psychologists who study how people become experts have focused much of their attention on feedback and what constitutes especially effective feedback. For girls and women to achieve their potential, they have to become experts. People don't become experts by chance—it is the result of what they learn, how they learn, their motivational systems, the feedback that they receive, and a host of other factors. Feedback is one area in which teachers have an especially good opportunity to make a difference. Good feedback has four characteristics that often are overlooked in educational settings:

1. *Refocuses selective attention* mechanisms on the appropriate aspects of a problem;

2. *Is process feedback* rather than simply feedback about outcomes;

3. *Disconfirms* wrong hypotheses and assumptions;

4. *Corrects faulty self-assessment.*

In the discussion of Strategy #9, you will learn how to refocus selective attention mechanisms. Under Strategy #2, you learned the importance of feedback to correct faulty self-assessment and how to use disconfirming evidence. Strategy #6 focuses on avoiding negative messages when you give feedback. In this section, we will focus on process feedback and encouraging students to seek feedback.

In order for people to learn from feedback, they have to have a large amount of it. This, we've learned, can be a problem for girls. One important change for teachers to make is to be sure that girls receive as much feedback as boys. Feedback, however, usually comes in the form of information about a student's performance, which can be threatening to students. Girls, more than boys, tend to be hypersensitive about criticism. Students, however, can also learn from models and mentors. In this case, the feedback is "disguised;" rather than focusing on *students'* performance, the lessons learned focus on the *model's* performance. Feedback is also threatening because it is usually accompanied by evaluation. But learning from a role model's mistake removes the threat, reducing defensiveness. This means that using your own experiences or relating those of others is an excellent way of providing feedback without having to work through students' defensiveness. You want to be sure to model how you seek and use feedback. When discussing stories about other role models, look for opportunities to discuss the feedback that they received and how it improved their performance.

Process feedback is given about the process rather than the outcome of performance. It's usually given during the process rather than afterwards. *Process feedback is much more useful than outcome feedback.* Imagine trying to learn to play the piano with only outcome feedback. The teacher would clap or boo at the end of your piece. You wouldn't know what, in particular, was good or bad about your performance. Think again about the chess players doing the post mortem. They are receiving feedback about the process. Players who forego the post mortem receive only outcome feedback: did they win or lose? It's no surprise that those with only outcome feedback don't improve as much or as fast as those with the process feedback.

Outcome feedback often comes in the form of reward or punishment. This means that it is closely tied to evaluation, which, as discussed, can be threatening. If we think of outcome feedback from the point of behaviorist psychology, positive outcomes result in reinforcement. In the "old days" of psychology, teachers were urged to reinforce students for desired responses. This is not a bad idea, but it doesn't go nearly far enough. Simply reinforcing outcomes is not the most efficient way to teach. Students need feedback on the *process.*

There are other problems with the technique of simply reinforcing students for desired outcomes. I've always been bothered by the notion of "social reinforcement." The idea is that teachers should use smiles, pats, and nice comments as reinforcers. But in order for reinforcement to be effective, it must be used only when the student enacts the desired behavior. If, for example, I'm reinforcing my toddler to use the potty by giving her "M&M" candies when she's successful, I don't want to give her the candy at any other time. That would only confuse her. If, then, teachers are really going to use smiles, pats, and nice comments as reinforcement, they should withhold them at other times. I can't think of anything more awful than a classroom in which the teacher is nice to the students only when they perform well academically! (Unfortunately, there are classrooms like that.) What students—all students—need is *positive regard* rather than social reinforcement. They need smile, pats, and friendly behavior because the teacher likes *them,* not because they scored "100" on a spelling test. Friendliness shouldn't be contingent on academic performance. Teachers should smile and be friendly not only when a student performs well, but at other times, too. *Give positive regard rather than social reinforcement.*

This confusion between positive regard and social reinforcement is a particular problem for girls. They come to believe that teachers like them because they're good, docile students. That means they have to maintain that performance to continue being liked. What teachers need to convey to girls is that they are liked because they're great kids and not because they make good grades or behave well. The feedback that they receive about academic performance should be separate from social rewards because girls need to learn to separate tasks from relationships. They need to see that relationships can be maintained even if their performance is not always perfect. Classrooms need to separate tasks and relationships so that students will learn to differentiate between them.

Feedback should be business-like and separate from the student–teacher relationship. Every student should receive feedback, not just those who perform poorly. In some classrooms, feedback equals criticism. Given that girls fear criticism, they will not be open to feedback. If the only feedback that students get is negative, then who wants feedback? So be sure your feedback includes as much positive as negative information. I tell my students that lots of notes on their papers doesn't mean that it's a bad paper; it means it was interesting and stimulated a lot of thought and comments.

The teacher is not the only source of feedback. Peers can provide feedback. Feedback also comes from the task itself when students are skilled at self-assessment. Students need to learn to seek additional feedback. *Teach students how to seek feedback and help.*

Help-seeking is psychologically complex. Consider the "I need some help" situation.[7] There are several ways to ask for help. Sometimes people try acting pathetic ("I'm desperate, please help") or act as though people ought to do things for them because they're important. The latter will make people dislike and resent women, although it's acceptable behavior for men in positions of power. The pathetic form also may work, but has some very negative long-term implications. (Unfortunately the pathetic form is one that is more common and more acceptable among women.) Being perceived as pathetic does not lead to positive expectations.

Asking for help is sometimes seen as a sign of weakness or inferiority, which can then fulfill someone's stereotypical expectation. This presents a serious problem for minority boys as well as for girls. A minority male student may need help but not be willing to admit it for fear of appearing stupid and thereby fitting a prejudiced person's negative stereotype. Teachers then assume a student doesn't care because he "didn't bother" to ask for help.

The kind of feedback that a teacher gives is one way to communicate expectations, which we know influences students' performance. Suppose a teacher expects a student to do well. The teacher then gives the student a lot of encouragement and support. He asks the student tough questions and gives effective feedback. The teacher's expectation has been translated into teacher action that will contribute to the student's success. The student tries harder because of the teacher's interest and attention. Look at the examples in the Exhibit and identify (1) the teacher's expectation and (2) what the teacher might do as a result of the expectation that could result in a self-fulfilling prophecy.

EXHIBIT

Steve's older brother was in your class and one of the very best students you've ever had. What do you expect from Steve? How might you behave toward Steve?

Expectation _____

_____

Possible teacher behaviors _____

_____

_____

Amy says she doesn't like math and has done poorly on the first exam.

Expectation _____

_____

Possible teacher behaviors _____

_____

_____

Susan's mother is a local artist whom you admire. Susan arrives at school with a tee shirt from a local art show. She tells you that art is her favorite subject.

Expectation _____

_____

Possible teacher behaviors _____

_____

_____

Look back at what you wrote. Did you identify teacher behaviors that were likely to make the expectation a self-fulfilling prophecy? The trick is to identify your expectations *before* you begin to act in ways that will make them come true. Practice in real-life situations, thinking consciously about your expectations. Being aware of expectations is the first step toward avoiding differential treatment of students. You'll find that if you can control your expectations, you'll succeed in eliminating most gender inequity in your classroom.

STRATEGY 6: AVOID NEGATIVE MESSAGES

Teachers send negative messages in a variety of ways. Excessive praise for mediocre work sends a "low-ability" message, too much sympathy coupled with low expectations and external attributions can send a "victim" message, or offering premature help can suggest low expectations. Nonverbal communication can send messages, too. A friendly pat can be encouraging. A sympathetic pat can suggest, "You poor dear." Listening attentively suggests that the listener values what the speaker has to say; ignoring or not calling on a student can suggest that the student doesn't have much worth contributing. Following up a student's comment enthusiastically builds self-esteem; quickly moving on to other topics suggests that the comment had little value.

The best way to avoid negative messages is to avoid negative expectations. Teachers' expectations lead them to give feedback that can convey negative messages. Teachers' expectations also contribute to different climates. Typically, teachers will create warm, supportive environments for favored students whom they expect to succeed. Such expectations result in quantitative differences in both input and output. Teachers teach more to students from whom they expect more. They cover more material, as well as more complex material. When teachers expect more, students are given more opportunity to learn and to meet expectations. Output also increases with increased expectations because teachers demand more from students from whom they expect more. They ask more questions, require better answers, pursue points longer, and so forth. This, in turn, ensures that the student will produce more.

When a teacher wants to help a child, but has low expectations for that student, the teacher often misuses praise. Remember, for praise to be effective, it has to be for a challenging task done well. Praise for a trivial task sends a "low-ability" message. If you praise a girl or a woman and she responds, "Oh, anyone could have done it," stop and think! If anyone really could have done it, why are you praising her? Your inappropriate praise suggests that you think she's not capable of much. *Learn to use praise effectively.* Effective praise must be sincere and must be for something praiseworthy. Students learn to discount insincere praise.

Praise tells students what we value. If we praise girls and boys for different things, we tell them that we value different skills and attributes for boys and girls. As we've seen, girls are often praised for being cute, quiet, or docile. Boys are praised for getting the right answer or for being independent. Be sure you give girls and boys "equal praise" for "equal work."

Teachers sometimes use praise to "build self-esteem." This confuses cause and effect. Self-esteem is the result of doing well; but rarely is it the direct cause. Telling a student that she's wonderful may make her feel good for a moment, but it's not likely to teach her algebra. High self-esteem doesn't magically result in algebra skill. But teaching her algebra and praising her legitimate achievement will boost her self-esteem. Telling students that they can "do anything they want to" doesn't build lasting self-esteem if they can't read well enough to get a job or get into college. To build their self-esteem, *teach* them *how* to "do anything they want to."

Praise is not always reinforcing. Sometimes public praise embarrasses students. Adolescent boys may find public praise to be a punishment. When he was in the ninth grade, my son came home livid about his horrible teacher who praised him in front of the whole class—causing him deep and lasting humiliation. That, he told me, was the last time he intended to turn in the best paper.

Because of the strong influence of behaviorism in psychology, teachers are often led to believe that praising or "reinforcing" students is the best way to motivate them. As we learned when discussing good feedback, it's not that simple. Praise is not like an M&M candy. Everybody likes candy and it can be an effective reinforcer for almost everyone. It doesn't matter whether the M&M itself is sincere or not. Praise, however, gets *interpreted* by students and may send a very different message and have a very different effect than the one intended by the teacher. Besides being sincere and spontaneous, praise should be contingent on behavior which the child controls. Too many teachers go around the room saying, "Good job," without really looking at what the student has done. Praise should be specific—tell the student exactly what's being praised, emphasizing the skill and attributing success to effort and ability. Rather than simply saying, "Great," say, "Great. You've really mastered dividing fractions. You've worked hard and it shows." Praise should be personalized. If everyone gets the same smiley face, it's not worth much.

Girls sometimes get "hooked on" praise. If a girl is not able to assess her own work and has received praise for her appearance rather than for her performance, she may crave feedback to reassure herself that her performance is okay. If in her classroom, the boys are taken more seriously, she may need praise to feel valued. If she also undervalues her own success and sees it as a fluke, she'll need the reassurance of external praise. If she further defines herself in terms of her relationships with others, then praise means the teacher likes her. This neediness is not healthy. Teachers need to build girls' self-confidence, teach them self-assessment skills, and retrain their attributions so that they can learn independently and enjoy intrinsic rewards.

Women and girls receive other "low-ability" messages in the form of compliments. Consider the following situation, in which a well meaning boss is trying to praise a woman: John introduces the staff to the new client, giving simply names and titles for the men while lavishly praising Mary's work when he introduces her—the client gets the message that "believe it or not, pretty little Mary can do her job." Teachers sometimes do the same thing by singling out a girl in a math or science class and "over-acknowledging" her, suggesting that it is a major surprise that she is there and able to do the work. Compliments are a good way to show interest in your students and to express positive regard, but you must beware of possible negative messages. Keep track of the compliments that you give students for a day or so. Do you give equal numbers and equal kinds to boys and girls? Are there hidden implications in any of the compliments? Beware of back-handed compliments, such as the one Mary's boss gave her. For more on this subject, read what Jere Brophy and others have described as behaviors that teachers use with low-ability versus high-ability students.[8]

EXHIBIT

Teacher Behavior toward Students with Perceived Low Ability	Boys	Girls
1. Waits less time to answer question.		
2. Gives students the answer rather than hints or rephrasing the question.		
3. Rewards inappropriate or incorrect answer.		
4. Criticizes for failure.		
5. Seats student farther away from teacher.		
6. Gives short explanation.		
7. Accepts inaccurate responses.		

EXHIBIT

Teacher Behavior toward Students with Perceived High Ability	Boys	Girls
1. Long wait to answer question.		
2. Gives hints or probes for correct answer.		
3. Interacts with or pays attention to.		
4. Praises for success.		
5. Gives feedback.		
6. Calls on to respond to question.		
7. Seats close to teacher.		
8. Gives long explanation.		
9. Smiles more.		
10. When grading, gives the benefit of the doubt.		

Think about the following situation.

Sally makes the honor roll, is elected to numerous school offices, volunteers in her community and gets remembered in the yearbook as the "Senior Class Cutest Girl." What negative message is being sent? By now, you can probably easily identify negative messages. Focus on the next (and harder!) step: what more appropriate message might you, as a teacher, send?

Negative message: _____

_____

_____

_____

Alternative message: _____

_____

_____

_____

In this case, for example, Sally is being sent messages that say that the hard work, dedication, and talent that went into her other accomplishments are of lesser importance than her cute appearance. Her reward—an acknowledgement in the yearbook—is based on behavior over which she has little control, her appearance. As her teacher, I'd want to assure her that when it really counts (college admissions and scholarships, jobs, etc.), her accomplishments will be very important. I'd want to use this chance to talk with Sally about the silliness and the sexism in this episode. I'd want to be sure that Sally feels good about her legitimate successes and doesn't feel that they have been denigraded. Now, try analyzing the following examples.

EXHIBIT

Kristi fails algebra. The teacher tells her not to feel bad. She tried hard and that's what matters. She can just take Arithmetic 9 next year. Girls don't need math and besides boys don't like smart girls.

Negative message: _____

_____

_____

_____

Alternative message: _____

_____

_____

_____

"That's a difficult problem, Sue Ann. See if James can help you with it."

Negative message: _____

_____

_____

_____

Alternative message: _____

_____

_____

"That's an excellent point, Dwight. Let's write that on the board so we can return to it. Now, Carrie, we don't have time to get off track. Make your point so that we can move on."

Negative message: _____

_____

_____

_____

Alternative message: _____

_____

_____

_____

Melissa missed a problem on the board and Ms. Gates asks someone else to do it, not wanting to embarrass Melissa by having her try it again.

Negative message: _____

_____

_____

_____

Alternative message: _____

_____

_____

_____

Because girls often don't do well in science class, the teacher asks them the easier questions to boost their self-esteem.

Negative message: _____

_____

_____

_____

Alternative message: _____

_____

_____

Because girls often don't do well in science class, the teacher is careful to always assign a boy as a lab partner. He suggests that if the girls are squeamish, to let the boy do the dissecting.

Negative message: _____

_____

_____

_____

Alternative message: _____

_____

_____

The teacher always makes a point of saying something personal and nice to each student every day. As the students file in, she says, "I'm anxious to hear your report today, Bill." To Sylvia, she says, "Oh, don't you look sweet today!"

Negative message: _____

_____

_____

Alternative message: _____

_____

_____

_____

"Students," says the teacher, "I need a big strong boy to help me."

Negative message: _____

_____

_____

Alternative message: _____

_____

_____

_____

"Judy, stop being so loud! Act like a young lady."

Negative message: _____

_____

_____

Alternative message: _____

_____

_____

The teacher asks a question and, as usual, the girls' hands shoot up, while the boys don't even seem to be paying attention. After a long wait, Tim raises his hand and the teacher quickly calls on him.

Negative message: _____

_____

_____

_____

Alternative message: _____

_____

_____

The principal visits the advanced physics class, in which there are only three girls. The teacher makes a point of introducing each girl by name and remarking that they are all doing just fine.

Negative message: _____

_____

_____

_____

Alternative message: _____

_____

_____

_____

Tom makes an error and the teacher corrects him and then gives him another, similar problem. Jessica makes an error. The teacher smiles and says, "Okay, let's go on. What about you, Jean, do you know the answer?"

Negative message: _____

_____

_____

Alternative message: _____

_____

_____

_____

At preschool, Sam is crying. The teacher tries hard to figure out what's wrong. Beth is crying and the teacher says, "Oh, poor little Beth. Do you need a hug?"

Negative message: _____

_____

_____

Alternative message: _____

_____

_____

_____

Libby goes into the high school guidance counselor's office to talk about her courses for next year. Despite her high grades, the counselor doesn't suggest that she take calculus or physics in her senior year.

Negative message: _____

_____

_____

Alternative message: _____

_____

_____

_____

Reginald is a 14-year-old African-American student from a housing project. He hasn't been doing his homework, so his teacher says, "I know things are real rough for you. If you can't do your homework, that's okay. I don't want to make things any harder for you. Just do it when you can."

Negative message: _____

_____

_____

Alternative message: _____

_____

_____

_____

STRATEGY 7: RETRAIN ATTRIBUTIONS

Although in general there are gender differences in how children explain success and failure, not all girls suffer from dysfunctional attributional styles and not all boys enjoy healthy attributions. The best way to find out how to help individual students is to talk to them about success and failure. Ask students to tell you (or to write) about a time when they were successful and a time when they failed. Probe to find out how they felt, what they believed was the cause of the success or failure, and how people reacted to their success or failure.

I ask my college students what others say about their academic success. While many women do report that significant others are supportive and positive, others report ego-damaging comments, such as "A lot of people must have done well," or, "Why can't you do well in *all* your courses?" Many comments from husbands or significant others are of the "that's great, but . . ." variety. "That's great, but what about all the time the kids spent with a babysitter?" Or, "That's great, but what about next semester when I'll be busier at my job and won't have time to help with the housework?" Or, "That's great, but it's only a class."

It should come as no surprise, that the same women downgrade their success. "I only did well because the test was unusually easy," or, "I did well on this exam, but it's not important." Sometimes, I ask women to tell me about a time when they were successful in their jobs or in their academic careers; then to tell me about a spouse's or significant other's success. Again, the same patterns emerge: some women trivialize their successes and attribute their success to luck while aggrandizing their husband or significant other's successes. But even more worrisome is that women can instantly think of many examples of their men's successes and frequently have trouble coming up with any examples of their own.

Women's successes are often viewed as unimportant and exceptions to the general rule, while their failures are often viewed as important and representative of their low ability. Hence, the test is unimportant and "only a test" when a woman does well, but the test is important and "a measure of ability" when the woman does poorly. Thus, when a woman does poorly on an exam, her husband or significant other might suggest that she drop out of school; when she does well, she receives a back-handed compliment.

Even young children can tell you about their interpretations of success and failure. Consider the import of these comments.

"I spilled my milk yesterday and made a big mess 'cuz I'm clumsy. My Mom yelled at me. I spill things a lot."

This child sees an accident as resulting from a rather permanent and general characteristic of himself (clumsiness). He's likely to spill more things in the future. Further, his mother shares this interpretation. A teacher who hears this type of story should elicit more stories of mistakes to determine if this is the usual way this child sees his own failure. If so, this child needs attribution retraining to learn how to frame the situation more constructively.

> "I spilled my milk yesterday and made a big mess 'cuz I'm clumsy—my Mom cleaned it up and told me I won't spill so much when I get bigger."

Notice the difference in interpretation. The child attributed the failure to a general trait, clumsiness, but his mother corrected the attribution and explained that the reason was temporary. She also implied the reason had to do with his size rather than with him personally. This is an example of attribution retraining. If this child continues to receive these reinterpretations of his attributions, his motivation and self-confidence should improve.

> "I did real good at the doctor and didn't even cry when I got a shot. I was very brave and my dad said I was a big girl."

This child sees her success as resulting from general and permanent traits (she's brave), and her father shares her interpretation. She expects to continue being brave and big and have more success. This is a healthy attributional pattern.

> "I did real good at the doctor and didn't even cry when I got a shot. I was very brave but my dad laughed and said I almost cried. He said that big kids shouldn't even flinch."

In this case, the child displayed a self-confident, optimistic interpretation of her success. Her father, however, downgraded it and relabeled it a failure. If this is a general pattern, this child is at risk for serious problems with self-confidence. A teacher could help restore her self-confidence with attribution retraining.

> "I left my toys on the stairs and my mom almost fell down. She said I made a bad mistake and punished me. I felt real bad and told her I wouldn't do it anymore. It was just that Samantha came to play, and I forgot and had to go to bed. Mama said I usually remember, but must try hard to remember all the time."

This child sees her mistake as an isolated case and not the result of a general character flaw. Her mother, too, saw it as a specific case. Neither the child nor the mother predict future mistakes based on this one episode. This is a healthy way to view a mistake.

> "I left my toys on the stairs and my mom almost fell down. She said I made a bad mistake and punished me. I felt real bad and told her I wouldn't do it anymore. It was just that Samantha came to play, and I forgot and had to go to bed. Mama said that was no excuse and I'm a bad girl and always leave stuff out."

Here the child saw her mistake as a slight blemish in an otherwise good record. She acknowledged her mistake and vowed not to do it again. While appropriate for her mother to punish her, her mother erred by explaining the mistake as resulting from a permanent and internal cause—she's a "bad" girl. This child, too, is a candidate for attribution retraining.

> "I got a trophy for soccer. It's gold and shiny and has a little soccer ball on top. My dad says they give them to all the little kids and not to expect one when I play next year with the big kids. I'd like to get another trophy but I probably won't."

This child has downgraded her success. The trophy doesn't count because everyone got one. She has been taught to see this trophy as resulting from external factors rather than from her own efforts. And because the external factors are temporary, she doesn't expect continued success. Neither does her father. After a story like this, the teacher should elicit more success stories and see if there's a general tendency to downgrade her successes. This child will need to learn to enjoy her success more.

> "I got a trophy for soccer. It's gold and shiny and has a little soccer ball on top. My dad says they give them to all the little kids because we had all worked real hard and learned a lot. He says if I keep working at soccer I might get more trophies!"

Here the parent has linked success with effort and expressed optimism that continued effort could lead to more success.

"I was supposed to make a model of a DNA molecule. I tried and tried, but it didn't come out right. The teacher said I didn't try. I made another one. It took hours, but I still got some of the parts the wrong way. I told the teacher that it was hard for me because of my learning disability, but she said if I was learning disabled I shouldn't be in Honors Biology. I'm probably going to fail biology."

This scenario is from my daughter who has learned to compensate for her learning disability on most tasks. She occasionally has difficulty with certain spatial tasks. She tried to interpret this failure as an isolated case that was not entirely her fault. Her teacher, however, first saw it as a lack of effort and then took it as general evidence that she couldn't do the rest of the work in the class. My daughter then saw this failure on *one* part of the course requirements as predicting failure in the *whole* course.

Children with learning disabilities are particularly at risk for negative attributions. Often they do work hard and still fail. If teachers are aware of the effort, they may then attribute the failure to a general lack of ability. This is why it is extremely important that when you retrain attributions so that you don't simply urge students to "try harder." For an idea of how to better handle situations like this one, consider my daughter's experience with a geometry teacher.

"I think I understood the idea, but I was having trouble with the compass. I tried and tried but couldn't draw the circle right. When I tried to do the intersection, it ended up in the wrong place. My test paper was a mess and I got a bad grade. I talked to the teacher after school and she showed me how to do it. She was surprised at how hard it was for me. We talked about my learning disability. She hadn't had a student with that problem before and asked if I needed more time on the next exam. She also asked if there was anything else that I was having trouble with."

In this case, the teacher saw this as a *specific* problem, not as an indication of low ability or of low effort. She offered helpful advice so that this one failure didn't predict future failure. She also spent a good deal of time patiently teaching my daughter how to use the compass, rather than simply suggesting that she try harder or quit.

Sometimes children do try very hard and still do not succeed. In such cases, the worst thing that a teacher can do is attribute the failure to low effort or to suggest they "just work a little harder." Unfortunately, some of the materials on attribution retraining emphasize only linking performance and effort. Note that what I'm suggesting is different: *explain failure as narrowly and specifically as possible*. Emphasize specific and temporary explanations for failure. Focus on specific strategies to improve performance. When linking effort to failure, be very specific: exactly what kind of effort in what area. A global "try harder" message is not helpful. But assisting the student to find exactly where he or she needs to try harder and teaching the student the necessary skills is helpful. Learning-disabled students, as well as those from at-risk environments, are in danger of failing despite great effort. For example, students from impoverished neighborhoods may arrive in kindergarten or first grade lacking skills that the teacher assumes all incoming students will have. Teachers need to carefully assess students' level of functioning to be sure that they only are given tasks that they are capable of performing. If a child tries hard and still fails, the teacher needs to teach the necessary skills while maintaining a cheerful, optimistic manner. Skills build on other skills and it's the teacher's responsibility to know where to start. Rather than assuming the child who tries hard and still fails is "stupid," the teacher needs to acknowledge that the child was given the wrong task without adequate preparation. Teachers also need to seek help from guidance counselors and school psychologists for special cases.

Think about the different messages that the parents and teachers sent to the children in these stories. Think about the cumulative effects of negative attributions! With practice, you can tune in to students' attributional stories and offer them more healthy explanations. These are a few strategies which will benefit all students.

- Link effort and performance.

- Focus on success.

- Use success to predict future performance.

- Emphasize pervasive, permanent, and internal explanations for success.

- Emphasize specific and temporary explanations for failure.

- Offer hope after failure.

- Redefine failure.

- Focus on choices and control.

- Teach optimism.

The following Exhibit shows how teachers can retrain attributions.

EXHIBIT

ATTRIBUTIONS FOR SUCCESS AND FAILURE

Situation or Comment	Sample Teacher Response
"I'm so surprised—I got an A!"	"There was no surprise—you deserved your A—you worked hard and you're a good student." (*Link effort and performance*)
"I can't do anything right. I made another error on this week's math."	Everyone goofs once in a while. Look at all the things you did *right* this week. (*Focus on success*)
"I blew the test."	"That's too bad, but I bet if we look at your exam, we can figure out what you need to study." (*Failure = opportunity for growth*)
"I made a good grade, but it was an easy test."	"You made a good grade because you mastered the material. Lots of people thought that test was hard." (*Internal attribution after success*)
Student had not exerted much effort and performed poorly.	"You didn't do well on this test. You'd have done better if you'd worked a little harder on Chapter 7. Why don't you go over that again before the unit exam? I'm sure that will help." (*Link effort and performance; Offer constructive advice; Explain failure narrowly*)
Student worked hard and still performed poorly.	I know you worked hard and hard work is important for success. I'm proud of you when you try. But we need to find out why your performance doesn't reflect your hard work. Let's go through it and see if we can focus on areas where I can help you. If you work hard, you can bring your grade up on the unit exam." (*Offer constructive advice;*

(continued)

Situation or Comment	Sample Teacher Response
	Express optimism for the future; Express confidence in the student; Show positive regard through nonverbal behavior)
Student performed well after hard work.	"See! You worked really hard and your grade reflects that. I'm so proud of you. Be sure you schedule your time so that you can keep up the extra studying. I know you can keep that good grade." *(Link effort and performance; Predict future success)*
Student is able to perform well with little effort.	"You did a good job as usual, but I think we need to find something more challenging for you. Let's see if we can set a challenging goal for you. Think of what all you could do if you worked really hard! I keep thinking about how hard you work at your guitar lessons and how much you've improved this year." *Or,* You're very good in science. Have you read about Watson and Crick and how hard they worked to win the Nobel Prize? Maybe you'd like to read that while the rest of the class reviews for the next test." *(Link effort with even better performance)*
Student blames failure on teacher	"The test *was* difficult, but let's look at it more objectively. See, on question 1, I was looking for references to these two readings. You didn't mention either." After reviewing the entire test, "Now, let's think about what you can do to prepare for the next test." *(Specific feedback after failure; constructive help for the future)*

Notice how attribution retraining differs from praise after success. Rather than simply saying, "You did well," or, "Good job," the teacher offers an explanation for the success. This is particularly important for girls, who tend to downgrade their successes. Teachers and parents also downgrade girls' successes by not considering their activities important or by assuming that because most girls do well in school, it's not significant that a particular girl does well. When my children were young, people often asked them if they liked school. Both said yes. To my daughter's "yes," they replied, "That's nice." But my son's "yes" would elicit "ohs and ahs" about how wonderful it is to find a little boy who liked school. These kinds of differential reactions tell little girls that their good schoolwork is unimportant.

There are long-term effects of downgraded success. Feeling good about success helps sustain people through tough times. But women often don't get enough mileage from their successes. Success should be uplifting, but if it's seen as specific, temporary, and external, then it doesn't compensate for failures and times of nonreward. For many women the result is burn-out. Other women and girls need constant reassurance that they're okay. Schoolwork provides constant feedback in the form of grades, but later in the real world, women lose the "fix" of daily good grades that sustained them. With their successes only providing evidence of temporary worth, they quickly lose confidence. This is exacerbated when they haven't developed skills, such as self-assessment, that would allow them to evaluate their own work and reward themselves or enjoy intrinsic motivation. When possible discrimination is added to the formula, things look even worse. Even when a woman's performance is good, she may not receive a fair reward. So teachers must remember to attribute their students' successes to internal, permanent, and pervasive factors.

Another important aspect of attribution retraining is *focusing on choices and control*. When a student feels like a victim who has no choices, she is at serious risk for failure. Once a student says, "I'm a victim," she no longer accepts personal responsibility for her schoolwork. The result is a passive person who is an unlikely candidate for success.[9] Women more often than men feel a legitimate lack of control over their lives. (One example is the responsibilities involved in child care, which is usually considered to be the mother's problem. How much control can a mother have over when her children get chicken pox and can't go to their daycare? Again, how much control can a pregnant woman have over when she will go into labor? Who among us has managed to time childbirth for summer vacation? On a more general level, women and girls are constantly restricted by being told not to go places alone or after dark—unless they have a man along for protection.)

Not everyone has a wide range of choices, but everyone has some choices. Students don't have complete control over their lives, but they do have some. Part of your attribution retraining should include focusing on legitimate choices that students *do* have. One important outcome from attribution retraining is to gain a feeling of control.

It's also important to acknowledge times when the problem really is external and beyond the student's control. The trick is to not let a child believe failure is *always* outside his or her control. Bad things can and do happen to people through no fault of their own, but we want students in such situations to view themselves as survivors, focusing on the future and strategies for future success rather than focusing on past failures.

Before you're ready to tackle retraining your students' attributions, you should start with your own patterns. Answer the questions in the following Exhibit to get an idea of the extent to which you feel as though you have control over your life.

EXHIBIT

DO YOU AGREE OR DISAGREE?

1. When I get good grades it is because I worked hard.

2. My supervisor's evaluation of my work depends on his or her mood.

3. I have little control over what my children, pets, friends, or spouse do.

4. My hard work goes unappreciated.

5. The problems facing this community, company, family, or country are too difficult to solve.

6. I can usually meet my goals.

7. I don't know why my spouse, significant other, or friend, picked me.

8. I lucked out getting my job.

9. I like to know all the details before surgery.

10. In the end, people get what they deserve.

11. Life is a gamble.

12. My vote doesn't make a difference.

Of course, we are all controlled by both external and internal forces, but the more you recognize and use the control you have, the more successful you can be. If your locus of control is more external, your aim here should be to become more internally controlled. Feeling in control helps you to take control. If you answered "agree" to externally oriented questions (2, 3, 4, 5, 7, 8, 11, and 12) or "disagree" to internally oriented ones (1, 6, 9, 10), think about your answers. Why, for example, don't you believe your good grades come about because of your hard work?

One way to begin focusing on choices is to discuss a current problem. It can be a home, work, or school problem. Identify all the choices, then have others suggest additional options. Some people have many good choices; others have much more limited choices. But everyone has *some* choices. The trick is to focus on the choices. This is like the glass: do you see it as half full or half empty? When you see choices, they become the foreground and the obstacles become the background. But if you focus on the obstacles, you never notice the choices.

You might try asking students questions such as the ones you just answered. You may be surprised at their answers.

EXHIBIT

DO YOU AGREE OR DISAGREE?

1. When I get a good grade it is because I worked hard.
2. My grade depends on the teacher's mood.
3. When I play, I usually have to do what the other kids want to do.
4. My parents never notice when I do something good.
5. The harder I try, the worse I do.
6. I can usually do what I set out to do.
7. I don't know why my friends like me.
8. I feel lucky when I make a good grade.
9. I like games that require skill and not just luck.
10. If you goof off, you deserve a bad grade.

Were your students more internally or externally controlled? While it's good to emphasize choices and to see yourself as having control, having a very strong internal locus of control can also be problematic. If you are extremely internally controlled, you may need to remind yourself that some things are not under your control. Do you assume responsibility for everything that goes wrong? Do you engage in self-blame? The trick here is to focus on real choices and real areas of control while acknowledging that none of us can control everything in our lives. Even though there can be many uncontrollable factors, bringing the choices to the foreground helps us be more optimistic and to seize opportunities. Focusing on what we can't change is depressing and encourages helplessness.

When you talk with students, you need to keep returning to the issues of choices and control. Remember how selective attention works. People's natural tendency is to focus on limited choices, blocked opportunities. They have to force themselves to shift their attention to available choices and opportunities. You can help by reminding students to look for choices. If students are not looking for them, they may not even see obvious choices. Once their attention is focused on control and choice, however, they will see more control and other choices. Have you had the following experience? You buy a new car and suddenly you see the same car everywhere? This happens because now your attention is focused on that car and each one gets through your selective attention "filters." Changing your focus of attention allows you to see things you normally overlook. So one way to "see" more opportunity is to shift the focus of attention away from barriers to opportunities.

Below are some examples of the way you might talk to students about choices.

Student 1: I can't go to college because my parents don't have any money.

Teacher: That's not true. There are lots of scholarships based on financial need. You can also work and go to college part-time. That's what I did. Let's go talk to the guidance counselor for some other ideas.

Student 2: I can't study because my parents are always fighting and yelling. It's too noisy.

Teacher: I know that makes it hard. Do you have a Walkman? Maybe if you wore your headphones, you wouldn't be able to hear the fights. Or, maybe you could do some of your homework before they get home.

Student 3: It's hopeless. I'm going to fail.

Teacher: You will if you continue like this. But the way I see it, you have several choices. First, you can work with me after school every day and do some extra credit, or, second, your parents can hire a tutor, or, third, you can do nothing and repeat this course.

Student 4: I guess I'll just go the local community college. I don't have much choice.

Teacher: That might be your best alternative, but you have some other choices. There will be some representatives from different colleges at College Night next week. Why don't you talk with them?

Student 5: I don't want to do my worksheet.

Teacher: I can see that. You have two choices. You can do your worksheet now and then read your assignment or, if you'd rather, you could read your assignment first, then do your worksheet.

Student 6: I can't go on the trip to Washington, D.C., because it costs too much.

Teacher: The trip is six months from now. Maybe you could raise the seventy-five dollars? Let's see if we can come up with some ideas for how you could earn the money.

Notice in the many of the retraining examples that the teacher expressed optimism. This is another important part of attribution retraining: *teach optimism.*

False optimism is no help; what you're striving for is optimism combined with some real help or strategy to make success happen. Optimism, like praise, must be believable. Martin Seligman believes that just as some people have learned to be helpless, people can learn to be optimistic.[10] Optimistic people do better in life than pessimists. Optimists set higher goals and are more likely to achieve them. Other people like optimists more, too. Optimism is contagious; optimists are happy and they create happiness around them. We've talked about how interactions are colored by teachers' perceptions of students. Teachers respond more positively toward optimistic students.

Think about your everyday language. Do you convey a sense of optimism and hope? One of my children's teachers would not allow students to answer a question with, "I don't know." Instead they had to reply, "I haven't learned that yet." What a great way to focus on learning in an optimistic way! This one little phrase tells the class that they are all expected to learn and that's it's okay if you haven't learned something yet—you will soon.

Seligman offers some suggestions for teaching optimism. The basic idea is to find out the students' beliefs about a situation and then offer disconfirming evidence. You start by defining the situation in a narrow and specific rather than in a general way. Writing down what the student says and making a list of the student's beliefs is helpful and demonstrates to the student that you are taking what's being said very carefully and that it will undergo careful analysis.

An example will clarify: Nancy gets easily frustrated and at the start of every task, announces that she won't be able to do it. Today's lesson is on decimals and Nancy won't even open her book.

Teacher: You haven't learned how to add decimals yet. But that's okay, we just started working on it today. Is the problem that you don't know today's lesson?

Nancy: Yeah, I guess that's it.

Teacher: Tell me why you can't do it.

Nancy: Well, it's too hard.

Teacher: What else?

Nancy: I'm not smart.

Teacher: You think you're not smart in math?

Nancy: Yeah.

Teacher: Any other reasons why you can't do this?

Nancy: Yeah. I didn't do the homework assignment.

Teacher: Let's think about what you've said. First you said it was too hard. How do you know it's hard if you haven't tried?

Nancy: I just think it would be hard.

Teacher: If it were really too hard, do you think it would be in our book?

Nancy: I guess not.

Teacher: Yes, and do you think anybody expects you to know it all before we've even gone over it?

Nancy: I guess not.

Teacher: Besides, can't you do some things that are hard?

Nancy: Yeah, I did the hard problems in language arts yesterday. And I help take care of my little brother and that's really hard.

Teacher: Right! I've seen you do hard things, too. Remember when I got that pencil jammed in the pencil sharpener and I couldn't get it out? You pulled on it and it came right out! That was hard.

Nancy: Yeah. And I was the only one who could do five laps in PE!

Teacher: Now, you also said you're not smart in math. I know math isn't your favorite subject, but I think you're pretty smart in math. I just think it's not your *best* subject. When you're interested, you do smart things in math; like last week when you liked the story problems about going to the store, you did very well.

Nancy: Yeah, I guess I did. Maybe I'm not dumb all the time.

Teacher: You also said that you didn't do your homework. That might make you do worse, too. Right?

Nancy: Yeah.

Teacher: If you'd done your homework, do you think you'd be able to start learning this?

Nancy: Probably.

Teacher: So it seems to me, first, it's probably not that hard; second, you're not dumb; and third, if you had done your homework, you'd be ready to start with the rest of the class. What do you think you should do for tomorrow's class?

Nancy: I guess I should read the assignment and try harder.

Teacher: Good! I know you'll do better!

Always end on an optimistic note after you've debunked the students' bad reasons for the problem. If a student presents legitimate reasons for the problem, suggest useful strategies for dealing with it.

There's a lot to learn about attribution retraining, but once you become tuned into the sorts of attributions that people make and you practice correcting them, it will start to feel more natural. Don't think of it as something extra that you have to do. Instead, use your attribution-retraining language to substitute for the way you now talk to students about success and failure. Below are some questions to ask yourself to help diagnose your students' attributional problems. If you can't answer these questions, you need to do some data gathering and talk with your students more.

1. What are my students' expectations that their efforts will lead to successful performance?

   Are the students over-confident—or under-confident?

   Can they make sound predictions of performance on specific tasks? Or, do they operate on the basis of a global self-assessment (e.g., "I'm a lousy student")?

   When they do succeed, do they alter their future expectations for success?

2. What are my students' levels of ability? Are they accurate in their assessment of their abilities?

3. Do my students have adequate self-management skills? Do they know how to plan, study, control stress, find help and resources, manage their time, and set goals?

4. Do my students have an accurate idea of the amount of effort that is necessary for successful performance on each task? Do they adjust their effort on the basis of task difficulty, feedback, and so forth?

5. Do my students attribute their successes to ability, effort, or luck?

   Do they attribute their failures to ability, effort, or luck?

   Do they alter their attributions after feedback?

   Can my students accurately evaluate their own performance? Do they use feedback to change their evaluations?

6. Do students perceive a link between their performance and rewards? What extrinsic rewards do students receive for their successes? Do students value these rewards? What extrinsic rewards do they value?

7. What intrinsic rewards do students receive for their successes? What intrinsic rewards do they receive for performance in another domain in which they are more successful?

8. Are students satisfied with their current level of success? What level of success would be necessary for them to feel satisfied?

Besides giving the appropriate feedback, you'll want to talk with students about the attributions that they make and help them become more aware of the ways in which they explain success and failure.

So far, we've described attribution retraining as though it's always a one-on-one activity. Teachers can, however, tell stories with appropriate attributional messages to the entire class. For example, researchers showed college students a videotape stressing that poor performance is often caused by a lack of effort and that greater effort will not only improve performance on a specific task, but also will result in increased ability.[11] Students who were initially "externally" control-led—those who felt that circumstances rather than their own actions controlled their lives—improved significantly on later tests and homework. Teachers can also learn to model good attributional style when talking about their own lives. Consider these examples.

> "I'm going to take a course this summer. It's going to be hard, but I'm going to work hard and keep up on all the reading. If I do, I can learn a lot that will help me." *(Link effort and performance.)*

> "It took me a long time to graduate from college because I had to go part-time. I had my ups and downs, but I was successful more often than not. I'm not good at everything, but overall, I think I've been successful." *(Focus on success.)*

> "I was late today because I was in a little car accident. It was my fault, but I've been driving for fifteen years with no accidents, so I guess I can still say I'm a good driver." *(Focus on success; put failure in a larger context.)*

> "I'm so proud of myself, students. I've worked up to ten miles on my exercise bike. This proves to me that I can do it. By the end of the year, I'm going to add another ten!" *(Use success to predict future performance.)*

> "My ten miles show that I'm well disciplined and when I put my mind to it, I can do most things." *(Emphasize pervasive, permanent, and internal explanations for success.)*

This last example may have put you off. It sounds like this teacher is brag-ging. Bragging is sometimes acceptable for men, but women aren't supposed to brag. This puts them in a bind because their successes are also less likely to be noticed! Women and girls need to learn to brag a little. Bragging doesn't have to be in public; bragging can even be internal. This teacher may not want to brag at the faculty meeting, but *should* brag to herself and to her friends and family.

> "I didn't do well when I was in high school and took physics. I guess it was because in those days not many girls took physics, and I really didn't try as hard as I did in my other classes. Aren't you glad things have changed?" *(Emphasize specific and temporary explanations for failure.)*

This last scenario may sound out of character for a teacher. Some teachers rarely admit any shortcomings or mistakes! But if students are to learn how to deal with failure, they need to see it as something that happens to everyone—even teachers. And, they need to have someone model appropriate attributions after failure.

> "My dog lost in the dog show this weekend. But maybe if I train with him more, we can do better next time. He and I both are still pretty inexperienced at show work." *(Offer hope after failure.)*

> "I was given some good feedback at the dog show—it showed me some things we need to work on. These shows are good because they help me pinpoint what I can do to improve." *(Redefine failure as diagnostic and as an opportunity for growth.)*

Here, the teacher is modeling nondefensiveness about feedback. This kind of talk can have a powerful impact on students who feel that adults are always evaluating them or that adults are not held accountable for their mistakes. Teachers could also talk about aspects of adults' lives that are similar to those of students, for example, a spouse graduating from law school who is nervous about the bar exam, or the example below.

> "I have to take two more courses to get my certification, but I get to choose which ones and whether to take one this semester and one next semester or take them both this summer." *(Focus on choices and control.)*

Retraining negative attributions and reversing negative messages require improved feedback, better role modeling, and changes in classroom materials and climate. Teachers need to get students discussing success and failure and what it all means. Failure is not just something that teachers do to students; it's a part of everyone's life. Success is not just something that happens to lucky people. Because adults like to sound in control, they rarely model to students how to deal with failure. You don't need to reveal any deep, dark secrets about your inadequacies, but it won't hurt to let students know that adults have to work to succeed.

Once you begin thinking about attributions, you should notice lots of examples. Share these with your students. One situation that I observed is particularly interesting in that it clearly demonstrates the differences between sympathy and attribution retraining. It also demonstrates how much more useful attribution retraining is.

I was in a meeting in which we were discussing the relative importance of teaching versus research in universities. A woman stood up and talked very passionately about having been a temporary instructor for eighteen years and how she had been exploited and underpaid. This all went to show how, in her view, teaching is undervalued and how her mistreatment demonstrates the wrong values held by universities. A successful and much-published female faculty member (we'll call her "Dr. Success") was deeply moved by her speech and later expressed her sympathies to both me and the "victimized" woman. Dr. Success assured "Ms. Victim" that it had just been a matter of luck that Dr. Success had been the successful one rather than Ms. Victim. Dr. Success wanted to help. But was this helpful? *No!* Dr. Success, unlike Ms. Victim, had completed her Ph.D., published good work, and applied to many jobs in order to locate a nontemporary position. Her success was not luck. What would have been helpful to Ms. Victim would have been to sit down with her and try to help her identify realistic choices and goals and to develop strategies to achieve her goals. Confirming her self-description as a victim with no choices was the worst kind of help. People who want to help others often make this very mistake—they offer sympathy and feed into a victimization story.

Consider another interaction I witnessed recently. Two female students were discussing their chemistry class. One woman complained about how much time she had put into her lab report and she still hadn't received a good grade. Her friend replied, "Oh, you know you didn't have to put in that much time. And you didn't follow the directions. You can't expect to get an A if you don't follow the directions." The disgruntled woman went on to complain about how the instructor disliked her. Her friend replied, "He's just not real friendly. He treats everyone that way." The conversation continued with the friend debunking each and every excuse offered. Then the friend offered a series of constructive suggestions, such as joining a study group, not missing so many classes, and paying more attention to instructions. Now this is the kind of friend we all need! This friend helped the other woman to see the situation realistically and offered concrete suggestions for change. I hope this helpful friend is planning on becoming a teacher!

Students, like the rest of us, can all use a little sympathy now and then, but mostly they need real help. We need to change students' dysfunctional attitudes and increase their competency. Feeling sorry for them or letting them feel victimized won't help them succeed. Sympathy is fine; but just don't stop there.

Consider the students described in the following Exhibit. See if you can determine their attributions, then write down feedback that you might give them to disconfirm their beliefs or to retrain their attributions.

EXHIBIT

Situation

"I made a bad grade because the test was too hard."

Student's Attributions

☐ permanent
☐ temporary
☐ general
☐ specific
☐ internal
☐ external
☐ ability
☐ effort
☐ luck (bad or good)

Possible response to disconfirm or retrain attributions

_____

_____

Situation

"I made a bad grade because my brother took my book and wouldn't give it back."

Student's Attributions

☐ permanent
☐ temporary
☐ general
☐ specific
☐ internal
☐ external
☐ ability
☐ effort
☐ luck (bad or good)

Possible response to disconfirm or retrain attributions

_____

_____

(continued)

Situation

"I made a bad grade because I can't understand math. I'm just lousy in math."

Student's Attributions

- ☐ permanent
- ☐ temporary
- ☐ general
- ☐ specific
- ☐ internal
- ☐ external
- ☐ ability
- ☐ effort
- ☐ luck (bad or good)

Possible response to disconfirm or retrain attributions

_____

_____

_____

Situation

"I made a bad grade because I didn't understand chapter four."

Student's Attributions

- ☐ permanent
- ☐ temporary
- ☐ general
- ☐ specific
- ☐ internal
- ☐ external
- ☐ ability
- ☐ effort
- ☐ luck (bad or good)

Possible response to disconfirm or retrain attributions

_____

_____

_____

Situation	Student's Attributions
"I made a good grade because I studied more than usual. But I probably won't do as well on the next test."	☐ permanent ☐ temporary ☐ general ☐ specific ☐ internal ☐ external ☐ ability ☐ effort ☐ luck (bad or good)

Possible response to disconfirm or retrain attributions

_____

_____

_____

Situation	Student's Attributions
"I made a good grade, but most people did. Besides, it was only a quiz and doesn't count much."	☐ permanent ☐ temporary ☐ general ☐ specific ☐ internal ☐ external ☐ ability ☐ effort ☐ luck (bad or good)

Possible response to disconfirm or retrain attributions

_____

_____

_____

(continued)

Situation	Student's Attributions
"Yeah, I made a high score on my SAT, but I'm just good at those kinds of tests."	☐ permanent ☐ temporary ☐ general ☐ specific ☐ internal ☐ external ☐ ability ☐ effort ☐ luck (bad or good)

Possible response to disconfirm or retrain attributions

_____

_____

_____

If you start talking in the classroom about attributions, you will be surprised to see how quickly your students pick up on the idea. Soon they, too, will begin to "retrain" each other. After a while, it will become a part of your classroom culture.

STRATEGY 8: REDUCE STEREOTYPICAL THINKING

Stereotypes are just categories, and the human brain thinks in terms of categories. We're wired that way. Stereotypes, then, are the result of the way in which all humans process information. Stereotyping is not something that only "bad" people do and it would be naive to think any of us could stop using stereotypes. As discussed earlier, not all stereotypes are negative. We also use positive stereotypes. Our goal in this section is to learn to recognize when we're using both negative and positive stereotypes and to *question our stereotypes by seeking more information about individuals.* Students can easily grasp the concept of a stereotype and enjoy finding them in books, on television, in cartoons, and in what the teacher says and does. This awareness is the best defense against harmful stereotyping.

Sex-role stereotyping also has to be considered from a developmental perspective. Preschoolers are beginning their quest for gender identity. They are aware of anatomical differences and are eager to learn what it means to be a boy or a girl. They are beginning to define for themselves the abstract categories "male" and "female," but they're not yet skilled at abstractions. The emergence of stereotypes means that the child is beginning to learn abstract concepts, which represents an important intellectual milestone. We shouldn't be too alarmed by preschoolers' sex-role stereotypes. Just as when children first learn the word "dog," they may overgeneralize its use to all animals, when children first are learning masculine and feminine categories, they are apt to over-generalize. They may think, for example, that because men tend to be larger than women, they are also older, more powerful, have higher status, and are the boss. As in all examples of concept learning, early concepts tend to be simplistic. Children pick up on society's stereotypes, assuming, for example, that women rather than men need to worry about "waxy yellow build-up" on kitchen floors and dirty toilets. Later, the concepts are corrected. A common example is that of a female physician whose three-year-old daughter says only men can be doctors, based on her exposure to society's stereotypes. Her categorization is primitive and inaccurate. She's ignored obvious data that doesn't fit her category. Gradually she will take her mother into account and build a more sophisticated notion of who can be a doctor. This is analogous to the small child who has a simplified view of the animal world and thinks all furry animals are dogs. The child who says only men can be doctors at three years of age is not sexist. She is merely looking for a simple way to understand what it means to be male or female and has relied on the information available to her. When children first form categories, they assume categories don't overlap: men do one set of things and women do another set. Young children assume that each category has its own unique set of features: only dogs have fur and only fish can swim. It takes some more cognitive sophistication to develop categories that overlap and to accept that dogs can swim and that many animals have fur. We need worry about the doctor's daughter no more than about the child who thinks all furry animals are dogs. Later, that child will learn that there are lots of categories of animals that share the same furriness feature. Children have to learn that both dogs and cats can have similar features and that both men and women can have similar jobs. In both cases, more knowledge and experience will result in more accurate categories. With knowledge children learn to reject stereotypes. As educators, our job is to be sure they receive that knowledge.

What we sometimes call stereotypical thinking in very young children is really only highly simplified and primitive abstractions. What's more, these abstractions often defy logic. Question the girl who says only men can be doctors about her mother and she may reply, "Oh, she's not a woman; she's my mom." The relationship between stereotypes and behavior is not strong for very young children. A boy, for example, may tell you that boys can't play with dolls as he himself is playing with one. Very young children aren't bothered by logical inconsistencies, so they may not adjust their stereotypes when presented with contradictory evidence. But don't worry, it all catches up to them. The little girl whose mother is a physician will understand when she's ready. The problem is when girls aren't exposed to information that challenges society's stereotypes.

I suggest raising students' awareness of *all* kinds of stereotypes and not just negative ones. Sometimes classroom searches for stereotypes become witch hunts with students "nailing" anyone who says anything "sexist" or "racist." Then the finder-of-the-stereotypes feels smug and superior. The person who perpetuated the stereotype feels put down. Students sometimes get the impression that it's bad to show a woman working as a nurse or a homemaker in a story for example, because that's a stereotype. Yet there are lots of women who are nurses and homemakers and being a nurse or a homemaker is a good thing! Discussions about stereotypes often become emotional and some people will feel threatened. Parents in particular don't react well to being told that they shouldn't buy sex-typed toys, for example. When trying to reduce sex-role stereotyping, it's important to send positive rather than negative messages, such as urging parents to buy gender-neutral toys rather than *not buying* sex-typed toys.

Bringing students' attention to stereotypes and questioning them is good practice for critical thinking. Consider the following incident. When my son was eight or nine years old, a new boy moved into the neighborhood. The other boys in his age range were all Anglo-American and the new boy was African-American. I noticed when they played, no matter what the sport, everyone fought to have Reggie on their team. Reggie was about the least coordinated boy I'd ever seen. I wondered why they were so anxious to have him as a teammate—he never made a basket or a hit and always dropped the ball. I thought perhaps they were trying to make him feel welcome. When I asked, I was told they chose him first because he was the best athlete. I pointed to the obvious disconfirming evidence, but was told flatly that he had to be the best because he was, after all, African-American. Their stereotype was that all African-Americans are alike—great athletes. They fully knew that their own Anglo-American crowd varied; some were really good, some were really awful, and many were average. When evaluating their own group, they paid attention to the data. But when evaluating Reggie, they relied on their stereotype.

This incident offered a good chance to talk about stereotypes. The boys had been nice to Reggie, so raising the question of stereotyping was not critical of their behavior. What if, instead, the boys had refused to play with Reggie because of a *negative stereotype?* What if they had said he was dirty or stupid? A lesson on stereotypes would be in the context of disapproval of their behavior. It would be a reprimand. Obviously they would have deserved to be scolded, but it would not have presented the optimal environment for learning about stereotypes. They might learn not to say mean things, but they wouldn't have learned much about how to reduce reliance on stereotypes. They might have felt guilty or defensive. What if a teacher had made a public example of their rude behavior? Students will be much more open to discussions about stereotyping if it's not done in the context of "bad" behavior. Teachers can unwittingly create a backlash by only discussing stereotypes in terms of something that prejudiced people do to women or to minority people and then pointing a finger at someone who just said something stereotyped.

In the case of Reggie, students might be asked to explain the basis of their stereotypes—where are the data? If the answer is, "Everybody knows that," or, "That's what I saw on TV," then the teacher can discuss why television is not always accurate or how lots of people believe things that aren't true. Students who are tuned into self-evaluation can easily discuss how one might evaluate who is a good athlete, then look objectively at the data. This approach teaches students to make evaluations based on data rather than on stereotypes.

Once, when I was very pregnant, I got on a crowded bus and no one offered me their seat. I finally said something sarcastic to the young man in the seat nearest me, and he explained that he didn't want to stereotype me as a helpless pregnant woman in need of male protection. Fear of stereotyping kept him from gathering data to test his stereotype; he didn't ask me if I needed to sit down. If teachers make stereotyping into a "sin," then students will retreat from dealing with people for fear of saying or doing something that may be interpreted as stereotyped. It's better to challenge and then change stereotypes than to learn simply to "keep your mouth shut."

ACTIVITIES

One approach to teaching about stereotypes is to talk about the stereotypes that people hold and the evidence on which they base their stereotypes. Ask students how to go about gathering data to challenge stereotypes. A good example is to ask them to tell whether their parents have ever stereotyped one of their friends. Someone will tell you about a friend who didn't look or dress the way that her parents would have liked. Discuss first the basis for the parents' stereotype. Why, for example, would parents believe that teenagers with tattoos and pierced navels are evil or that girls with purple mohawks are fast? Then ask them what kinds of evidence would challenge the stereotype.

Discussing stereotypes outside the realm of sexism and racism will defuse some tension, so that it will be easier to talk about prejudice and hurtful stereotypes with your students. An important lesson to impart is that sexism and racism stem from ignorance. Students can easily see how lack of knowledge leads to wrong conclusions and how the search for knowledge can change the ways in which we think about people.

With older students, you might try soliciting adjectives that describe people who hold certain jobs and then discuss the stereotypes that emerge. Scientists, for example, are typically described as Anglo-American, somewhat nerdy, men over age forty, who wear white labcoats. Physicians are usually pictured as male, despite the fact that now most medical school classes have 40% women. Discuss the evidence for such descriptions and how such stereotypes limit opportunity. The advice columnist Ann Landers, for example, received a letter from a female medical student, who reported that when she told someone she was in medical school, the person remarked, "Oh, my sister's a nurse, too." How do such stereotypes affect people? Then ask students for adjectives to describe men or women in nontraditional roles. Do students supply negative adjectives to male nurse, male hairdresser, male ballet dancer, female construction worker, female engineer, or female lawyer? Discuss the implications of these stereotypes. Some suggestions for careers to discuss are listed below:

doctor	newspaper reporter
secretary	schoolbus driver
nurse	farmer
lawyer	mathematician
umpire	firefighter
principal	pilot
ballet dancer	police officer

scientist   dentist

business executive   accountant

kindergarten teacher   hairdresser

Marine sergeant   college professor

engineer   race car driver

To help students see how stereotypes can limit options, ask them to complete sentences such as those below. Then help students debunk the stereotypes.

A boy would never _____

Everyone would tease a boy who _____

Girls should not _____

Teachers expect boys to _____

Teachers expect girls to _____

Girls can't _____

Boys can't _____

Fathers don't _____

Mothers don't _____

Women shouldn't _____

Men shouldn't _____

Challenge Your Own Stereotypes

Teachers have stereotypes about students, which affect how they interact with them. Consider the descriptions in the box. What do you think these young people would be like as students? How popular would they be likely to be? Would they be good athletes? What kinds of interests would they be likely to have? Would they be likely to have behavior problems? What would their parents be like? Would you like this student? Would you be comfortable with the parents? Then think of what information you might seek to *disconfirm* your stereotypes.

EXHIBIT

Sam is from a broken home. His mother is a cocktail waitress and rarely attends PTA meetings.

My expectations: _____

_____

_____

_____

_____

Information that might disconfirm my stereotypes: _____

_____

_____

_____

_____

Dave is a tall, African-American boy who walks confidently and talks with self-assurance. His older brother was the star of the basketball team.

My expectations: _____

_____

_____

_____

(continued)

Information that might disconfirm my stereotypes: _____

_____

_____

_____

_____

Mary is a conventionally attractive adolescent, who is unusually well developed physically.

My expectations: _____

_____

_____

Information that might disconfirm my stereotypes: _____

_____

_____

_____

_____

Cassandra's parents are both artists.

My expectations: _____

_____

_____

_____

_____

Information that might disconfirm my stereotypes: _____

_____

_____

_____

_____

John's father is a physicist.

My expectations: _____

_____

_____

_____

_____

Information that might disconfirm my stereotypes: _____

_____

_____

_____

_____

Sam is very small for his age, wears glasses, and is very quiet.

My expectations: _____

_____

_____

_____

(continued)

Information that might disconfirm my stereotypes: _____

_____

_____

_____

_____

Pierre is from a family with a great deal of money, power, and status in the community.

My expectations: _____

_____

_____

_____

_____

Information that might disconfirm my stereotypes: _____

_____

_____

_____

_____

Ellen is very overweight.

My expectations: _____

_____

_____

_____

Information that might disconfirm my stereotypes: _____

_____

_____

_____

_____

Lance, a high school student, has shoulder-length hair, a tattoo, and an earring.

My expectations: _____

_____

_____

Information that might disconfirm my stereotypes: _____

_____

_____

_____

_____

Rachel is a cheerleader.

My expectations: _____

_____

_____

_____

(continued)

Information that might disconfirm my stereotypes: _____

_____

_____

_____

_____

Henry is a football player.

My expectations: _____

_____

_____

_____

_____

Information that might disconfirm my stereotypes: _____

_____

_____

_____

It's a math class and Tai Youn is an Asian-American boy.

My expectations: _____

_____

_____

_____

_____

Information that might disconfirm my stereotypes: _____

_____

_____

_____

_____

Sara is a fourteen-year-old girl who is pregnant and lives in a housing project.

My expectations: _____

_____

_____

_____

Information that might disconfirm my stereotypes: _____

_____

_____

_____

_____

Did you have expectations about these students? Some of your expectations may have been reasonable as first guesses. The problem comes when you're not open to new information because of your initial stereotype. You may start to seek information to confirm your stereotype. Let's say, for example, that you expect Henry, the football player, to be a poor student. You might notice his mistakes and discount his good academic performance. "He must have gotten help on this project," or "He got lucky." In Henry's case, a teacher ought to be consciously on the lookout for evidence that he's bright and academically capable.

I used to train people who interviewed prospective job applicants. One exercise I used was to have interviewers jot down their expectations after looking at the resume, but before they met the person. From their expectations, they had to frame questions that might *disconfirm* their expectations. Were you able to identify information that might challenge your beliefs?

My favorite story of teacher stereotyping involves my husband's kindergarten teacher. My husband is quite nice looking now and a successful philosophy professor. But back then, he had crossed eyes, a bad overbite, and one ear that stuck out. To make matters worse, no one realized he needed glasses, so he tended to be rather clumsy. His kind-hearted teacher told his parents not to expect much from the poor dear boy. The problem was not only the teacher's expectations. The big problem was that the teacher didn't go out of her way to test her expectation that he wasn't too bright. She should have sought information to *disconfirm* her expectations. Instead she focused on things that *confirmed* her expectations.

One of the most important tasks ahead of you is to identify your own biases and then work to disconfirm them. You may believe, for example, that girls aren't good in math. You are, after all, the product of your socialization. But being aware of this bias, you must focus on good math abilities that exist among your girls and take note of some of the boys' inadequacies. Over time, your bias should disappear! You've read about self-fulfilling prophecies. Often our biases are confirmed because we contribute to the process by seeking confirming data and ignoring disconfirming data. In this case, if you believe girls aren't good at math, you may prevent some girls from achieving in math by overlooking their ability, discounting their successes, not giving them effective feedback, and having low expectations for them. In this way, your stereotype may be confirmed. In fact, teachers who don't believe girls can do math usually have female students who do poorly in math.

Challenge Students' Stereotypes

Students also have stereotypes of themselves. Ask yourself, "Do my students see themselves as 'the kind of people' who should succeed academically? Does their view of their natural role conflict with the role of a successful student? Does their peer group or family see them in the role of a successful student?" When breaking down stereotypes, don't neglect self-stereotypes. For example, girls may not choose difficult courses because it violates their personal stereotypes. Students always have labels for different types of students. Ask them to define these words. Talking about the characteristics of "geeks, nerds, PIBs, (people in black), jocks, preps, buzz jocks, sluts, dorks, airheads, bimbos, tree huggers, Dead Heads, tricks, roadies, and skanky-thrash-punks," or whatever are the current categories, can be a useful way to heighten students' attention to stereotyping. Consider the following hypothetical classroom discussion.

Teacher: What's a "Dead Head"?

Student 1: Someone who's obsessed with "The Grateful Dead."

Teacher: So they are alike in that way. Any other ways?

Student 2: Well, they wear Grateful Dead tee shirts and stuff.

Teacher: Jason has on a Grateful Dead tee shirt. Are you a Dead Head?

Jason: Not really. I mean I like the Dead a lot, but I'm not like a fanatic or anything

Teacher: Tell me more about Dead Heads.

Student 3: A lot of them have long hair.

Teacher: Do all of them have long hair?

Student 3: No, but lots.

Teacher: Are all people with long hair Dead Heads?

Student 4: Of course not!

Teacher: So if I know someone's a Dead Head, how much do I know about them?

Student 5: Well, I guess not a whole lot. You'd know what kind of music they like, some of the things they like to do, and something about the way they're likely to dress.

Teacher: How did you guys learn about Dead Heads?

Student 6: From magazines and TV. And from people talking. But I don't really know any Dead Heads.

Student 3: My dad told me about some guys he knew in college who used to follow the Dead on concert tours.

Student 7: I guess we don't have much information to go on. Knowing someone's a Dead Head wouldn't tell me very much about him. I wouldn't want to predict what he'd be like, besides liking The Grateful Dead.

Ask students to list adjectives describing themselves, students of their own sex, and students of the opposite sex. Discuss the lists. Do students all use similar adjectives for boys? For girls? Do boys and girls see boys in the same way? Do girls and boys see girls in the same way? Are there adjectives that overlap for boys and girls? Do the self-descriptors match the same-sex descriptors? (There should be some overlap because stereotypes describe people in *limited* ways.) Why is there more variety among the self-descriptors? Does the boy or the girl list have more negative words?

Fight the Media

Once students are aware of stereotyping, ask them to bring in examples from books and the media. Advertisements and television commercials are an especially rich source of stereotypes. Find copies of old magazines. A *Life* magazine from the 1950s or 1960s will give students a sense of how stereotypes change or don't change over time. Then, as a class, have the students debunk the stereotypes. Keep the tone light and make this a fun experience.

Students will enjoy gathering data and analyzing it. Ask them to keep a record of the way in which men and women are portrayed on their favorite television programs or in commercials. You may want to design a form for their data collection, such as the one in the following Exhibit.

EXHIBIT

Program: _____

	Important Male Characters			Important Female Characters		
	1	2	3	1	2	3
Name						
Descriptors						
Job						
Activities						

Were there more male or female characters? Look at the adjectives that students recorded under "Descriptors." Do they reflect societal stereotypes? Are they negative stereotypes? Do men and women have different jobs on television? How are their activities different? Be sure that students display the results of their research.

Students may enjoy writing their own scripts by reversing the male and female columns. What would *Designing Women* be like if the main characters were all men? How would a female version of *Fresh Prince of Bel Air* work? A female *Doogie Howser? Major Mom?* What if the *Teenage Mutant Ninja Turtles* were girl turtles? Would a female duck with Donald Duck's personality be funny? If they reversed roles on *Who's the Boss?*, so that a man was a highly paid executive who hired a female housekeeper, would they still have to ask, "Who's the boss?"

If you ask students to analyze commercials, ask them to identify who has the problem and who has the solution. Do women usually have the problem, while men have the solutions? Why, if a woman has a dirty toilet, is there a male voiceover supplying the solution? Is it because men usually clean toilets? Television commercials are such a part of everyday life that many students are not aware of the messages that they send.

Your class could vote on a award for the funniest example of a sexist commercial. You might have a "No Comment" section of a bulletin board, where students can paste examples of print ads or cartoons that show stereotypes.

Model Gender-Neutral Behavior

Teachers can help break down stereotypes by simply breaking them. The male teacher who is warm and nurturant is breaking a stereotype. The female teacher who is assertive and strong is breaking a stereotype. Teachers of young children can model gender-neutral play. Female teachers can play with trucks and male teachers can feed baby dolls. With the exception of parents, teachers are the adults with whom children spend the most time, and seeing them display a wide range of gender-neutral behavior is one of the most effective ways to expand children's ideas about their own options for behavior. Finding stories and books about men and women acting in nonstereotypical ways or performing nonstereotypical activities is also a good idea.

Avoid Sexist Language

Much has been written about the need to use language that doesn't exclude or denigrate girls and women. Fire*man*, police*man,* and chair*man* all suggest men. Fire*fighter*, police *officer* and *chair* are all more inclusive. Using masculine pronouns can make girls and women feel excluded. A letter addressed, "Dear Sir," strongly suggests that the reader is male. A *"lady* doctor" or *"lady* artist" suggests someone who is not quite serious about her work, just as a "*gentleman* farmer" is someone who only plays at being a farmer. Using nonparallel terms such as "college *man*" and "college *girl*" suggests that males are more important or mature. "I now pronounce you, man and wife," suggests that the woman has changed roles but the man hasn't. A *bachelor* is simply an unmarried man; but an unmarried woman might be an *old maid* or a *spinster.* There's a *hen-pecked* husband but no *rooster-pecked* wife. Executives might ask you to call their "*girl*" to set up an appointment, but even if they had a male secretary, they would never say their "*boy.*" Men are *assertive;* women are *aggressive.* We are all bombarded with language differences that assert that women are not included, are not important, or have negative personal characteristics.

Teachers need to be alert to sexism in language and avoid sending negative messages through their language. Changing your language takes practice and, again, the first step is awareness. There are many good guides to nonsexist usage and teachers should gain skill at finding ways to avoid masculine pronouns and to create alternate phrases to replace sex-typed ones. Students also can learn to identity and correct sexist language.

Some of the reasons for nonparallel forms come from differences in status between men and women. As society becomes more equal, there will be little need for phrases such as "lady doctor" because being both female and a doctor will not be unusual. Language evolves as society evolves. Language reflects society. As society changes, so will language. Teachers need to be aware of and try to use nonsexist language, but an occasional slip of the tongue will not do serious damage. Saying "man hole cover" is unlikely to doom young girls to inferior status.

Value Things Feminine

While emphasizing nonstereotypical behavior, teachers sometimes send the message that anything feminine is of lesser value. Young women sometimes report pressure to go into male-dominated fields because they are told that female-dominated fields have low status. Women who choose to be homemakers feel they must defend their decision. I have a female colleague who was teased about making curtains for her office. I once had a high-powered interview in New York City and mentioned that I had two young children. The woman interviewing me sneered and said, "Oh, I didn't know people did that anymore." Gender equity doesn't mean traditional masculine attitudes, values, behavior, or interests are better! It also doesn't mean all young girls have to fit some new androgynous stereotype. Establishing a gender identity should include a chance to explore fully the whole range of feminine behavior. Teachers should not denigrate girls for behaving "like girls." Gender equity in the classroom does not mean an end to playing with dolls, the house-keeping corner, make-up, dresses, flirting, or giggling. It's about a wider range of choices for everyone.

Be sure to provide opportunities for boys to be nurturant and sensitive. Praise them for being sensitive, nurturing, good listeners, good helpers and other behaviors typically valued for girls.

Don't Tolerate Harassment of Girls

Because of some of our stereotypes of typical boy/girl behavior, we find it acceptable for boys to unmercifully tease and harass little girls. This often goes beyond good-natured fun. Do you remember the first girl in your class who developed breasts? Chances are she was called bad names, had her bra strap snapped daily, and was subjected to psychological abuse on a routine basis. It is common for children to tease each other, but learning respect for others should be a top priority. Children's insensitive behavior stems partly from their inability to appreciate other people's perspective. In preschool, teachers work on awareness that hitting others hurts just as much as being hit. This sensitivity training needs to continue so that cruelty, whether verbal or physical, is not tolerated. Too often, teachers overlook boys' cruelty to girls as "boys just being boys." Remember how "Millie" felt when the teacher stopped the teasing of the child in the wheelchair but did not stop the teasing of girls? Allowing boys to be cruel to girls sends the message that what happens to girls is not very important. When a girl complains of mistreatment, ask yourself how you would react if a minority boy or a child with a disability had brought the same type of complaint. The girl's complaint should receive the same consideration.

Similarly, music that denigrates and humiliates women should not be tolerated at school. Carefully monitor what gets played at school dances. Talk with students about song lyrics or album covers. Ask them about violence toward women and whether verbal assaults on women could contribute to physical assaults. Ask them to analyze some popular songs. Are men and women portrayed differently? Have students write out "the story" behind the lyrics and analyze it for stereotyping.

Stereotypes are dangerous because they block the gathering of information about individuals. They encourage us to shut down our thinking. We think we know all we need to about that person. Awareness and knowledge are the only defense.

STRATEGY 9: REDIRECT SELECTIVE ATTENTION

People aren't like computers. Computers can search all their memory banks, weigh each piece of information, and without any emotion or bias, arrive at a decision. We humans can't consider everything we've ever learned about a topic, weigh all possible alternatives and compare each alternative to every other alternative when we have to make a decision. We're limited in our processing capabilities. Much of the information available to us is not likely to be relevant to our immediate concerns—our brain is able to bypass all the "noise" because of *selective attention*. Prior experience tells us that not everything is important and that we should only let in information that will help us. This same selective attention process occurs for all humans in all kinds of situations. Experience and knowledge determine what will stand out as we go through life. Junior high school students' prior experience, for example, tells them that they need to attend to the brand of shoes that their friends are wearing, rather than to the algebra lesson. Cool shoes "pop out" at junior high students, while things that we adults think are important go unnoticed. The critical information (shoes) becomes the foreground and the less important information (schoolwork) becomes the background.

Based on vast experience and knowledge of "what's important or cool," adolescents naturally attend to what kinds of shoes other adolescents wear. They don't have to remind themselves to do this. They don't have to list all of the information coming in—algebra facts, the weather outside, chipped paint, teacher's clothes or hairdo, fellow students' shoes, and so forth—and weigh each to determine what is relevant. Their brain has learned to focus on shoes and ignore other information. That algebra information will most likely go, as they say, "in one ear and out the other." Adolescents do this because they are limited information processors, and they can't attend to and remember all of the complex information to which their senses are exposed. Nature solved this problem in humans by designing our brains so that, through experience, we learn to sort information into categories of "important" and "unimportant." Only the important information gets through.

Consider a telephone. See whether you can correctly label each key with the numbers, letters, and symbols (see Figure 3.1).

Chances are you were not able to do this correctly. The "1" key, for example, has no letters and there is no "Q." You've seen this information millions of times. Why don't you know it? Well, it's because your brain correctly decided that you don't need it—you never dial a phone unless there's a phone in front of you. You never had to consciously decide to ignore this information; your brain very cleverly determined that you should not waste your limited information processing capabilities on this information and didn't let it through. This selective attention phenomenon allows us to very quickly and efficiently sort through a huge

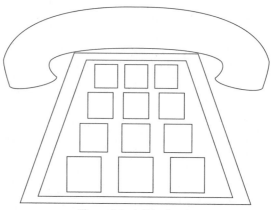

Figure 3.1 A Telephone.

mass of information. It sometimes, however, causes us to miss something that will turn out to be important.

The special problem for women and girls is that their attention is often not directed at some potentially important things, such as math and science. So teachers need to *focus attention on math and science*. What is selected to notice and remember is not random—it results from subjective experiences, which for men and women are very different. We can think of many examples. Have you ever heard a wife and husband both describe their vacation (the *same* vacation)? Sometimes you wonder if they were in the same place at the same time! One couple I know visits the same countries, but she sees mostly the plant life and he sees mostly the economic life. This selective attention phenomenon is powerful because it makes people exaggerate any differences, no matter how seemingly trivial. Small differences in socialization practices cause women and men to focus on different features of new situations, which then cause them to learn different things, which then influences future learning and so on. Because each new experience is seen through the filter of previous different experiences, the world looks more and more different as long as men and women continue to gain different experience.

This idea of selective attention is very important—we "see" what has been important in the past and tend not to notice things that have been irrelevant in the past. We can change what we attend to, but it takes serious effort. That's what education does—it focuses our attention on new things. Only after we've convinced our brain that those new things are important can we learn. This is why we can't teach unmotivated students—their brains don't think the material is important and these students don't tell their brains otherwise.

It's important to realize that we cannot attend to everything, no matter how hard we try—we have to rely on our automatic selective attention mechanisms because of the way our brains are made. We can, however, change what our brain thinks is important. Teachers can have a powerful influence on students by redirecting their selective attention processes. We've already talked about the importance of *directing attention to choices rather than to barriers.* Teachers often need to *redirect girls' attention to task-related information and redirect boys' attention to relationships* and how things will affect people. Teachers also need to redirect girls' attention to math and science. When girls' contributions are overlooked, teachers can *redirect attention back to girls' comments or work.* In classroom discussions, teachers control what receives attention. Putting girls in the forefront is one way to highlight their contributions. Something as simple as saying, "Let's return to a point that Latoya made earlier," can let the class know that you value Latoya's contribution. Finally, remember to *redirect attention to women's contributions to knowledge and culture.* Talk about female scientists, authors, and artists to demonstrate that women have contributed to the topic under study.

STRATEGY 10: REMEMBER INDIVIDUAL DIFFERENCES

Students are not just generic boys or girls. Gender differences and gender-role expectations interact with other social categories. Different cultures define gender roles differently; social expectations and behavior are influenced by socioeconomic status, parental education, and differences in ability and personality. But to understand what makes a student tick, teachers need much more information than simple demographics.

In America's schools, too many different cultures exist to make it feasible for teachers to become experts on all of them. It's somewhat dangerous to learn just a little about each because that encourages stereotyping. Instead, teachers should take these bits of information about different groups as examples of the variety of ways in which culture can affect learning. *The teacher's emphasis should be on finding out as much as possible about each student as an individual.* It's good to know, for example, that some cultures don't consider a girl's education to be a priority. Just don't assume, based on a particular student's ethnic background, that *her* parents will feel that way. It's also good to know that, on the average, girls are less interested in science than boys. Just don't assume, based on her gender, that a particular girl won't like science. Courtney Cazden and Hugh Mehan suggest that basic principles of anthropology and sociology, rather than details of various cultures, should be part of a beginning teacher's knowledge base.[12] What this book has taught so far are some basic principles of psychology. These principles give a general picture of why, on the average, there are achievement differences between men and women—and has provided lots of ideas on how to equalize opportunity in the classroom so that there will be fewer achievement differences in the next generation. But remember that these principles will work a little differently with each student.

As we've seen, giving feedback is complex; it's not enough simply to know whether the student is a boy or a girl. Two factors that obviously matter are the student's level of achievement and his or her ability level. *Teachers have to know where their students are and what they're ready to learn.* Personality matters, too. Some students enjoy competition and thrive in a competitive environment. Others become anxious and perform poorly in competitions. Some students love an audience; others prefer performing in private. Some students suffer from high anxiety; others are always relaxed. The anxious students don't respond well to pushing; the other ones do. Knowing who to push, and how and when, requires that you know the student well. Think of a really effective coach. He or she knows when to push and when to back off. Successful coaches know their players.

Finding out more about your students requires attention to their individual reactions. Watch (and take notes) when you have students engaged in a competitive activity. Who rises to the occasion and performs better than usual? Who becomes nervous? When you have students working in groups, who shines? Who assumes leadership roles in groups? Which students turn in better work when they're in groups? Look around during an exam. Who's working steadily and calmly? Who's agitated, fidgeting? Who hands in tests early and who late? Whose test performance is higher and whose lower than on other assignments? The student who under-performs on exams may be suffering from test anxiety, in which case suggesting that the student work harder to improve test grades is not useful feedback. *Be especially careful when suggesting more effort to be sure the student has the necessary skills.* Remember, too, to make feedback after failure as *specific* as possible: suggest effort on a *specific* task rather than suggesting that, in general, the student is lazy. Linking effort and performance *doesn't* mean telling a student that poor performance is the result of a general lack of effort.

Deborah Stipek provides some very useful checklists for identifying individual problems. The following Exhibit is a part of one of her checklists and focuses on work orientation (W) and confidence (C), two areas in which gender differences are often found.[13] She suggests, if possible, having two adults fill out the form to increase its accuracy.

EXHIBIT

Student's name _____

Put a number before each behavior:

  −1 = *not usually true*; 0 = *sometimes true*; +1 = *usually true*

1(W). _____ Pays attention to the teacher.

2(W). _____ Begins work on tasks immediately.

3(W). _____ Follows direction on tasks.

4(W). _____ Maintains attention until tasks are completed.

5(W). _____ Completes work.

6(W). _____ Turns assignments in on time.

7(C). _____ Persists rather than gives up when problems appear to be difficult.

8(C). _____ Works autonomously.

9(C). _____ Volunteers in class.

10(C). _____ Test performance reflects skills level demonstrated on assignments.

11(C). _____ Seeks help when it is needed.

12(C). _____ Not upset by initial errors or difficulties.

13(C). _____ Enjoys challenging work.

  (w) = work orientation; (c) = confidence

Scoring: Create scores by adding together all of the +1's and −1's in each of the two categories. A score close to or below 0 suggests that the student may have a problem that needs attention.

Source: Stipek, D. (1993). *Motivation to Learn: From Theory to Practice.* Boston, MA: Allyn and Bacon, pp. 273–274.

One individual difference which teachers need to be alert to is helplessness. We've discussed this in several places, and teachers need to be able to identify those children who really do feel helpless in school. Stipek's checklist for helplessness, presented below can be very useful.[14]

EXHIBIT

Instructions: Rate children who are not exerting much effort on school tasks and who appear to be performing below their capacity. Create scores (1) by summing all ratings and computing the average, or (2) by counting the number of "4s" and "5s." An average of 3 or above, or more than about five ratings of 4 or 5 suggest that the child lacks confidence in his or her ability to succeed and has given up trying.

	Never				Often
1. Says, "I can't."	1	2	3	4	5
2. Doesn't pay attention to the teacher's instructions.	1	2	3	4	5
3. Doesn't ask for help, even when she or he needs it.	1	2	3	4	5
4. Does nothing (e.g., stares out the window).	1	2	3	4	5
5. Doesn't show pride in successes.	1	2	3	4	5
6. Appears bored and uninterested.	1	2	3	4	5
7. Is unresponsive to teacher's exhortations to try.	1	2	3	4	5
8. Is easily discouraged.	1	2	3	4	5
9. Doesn't volunteer answers to teacher's questions.	1	2	3	4	5
10. Doesn't interact socially with classmates.	1	2	3	4	5

Source: Stipek, D. (1993). *Motivation to Learn: From Theory to Practice.* Boston, MA: Allyn and Bacon, p. 283.

It's important to use a device such as a checklist to ensure your objectivity. Otherwise you may fall back on your stereotypes and assume that a girl lacks confidence or is helpless simply because she is a girl.

Test anxiety is a good example of how attribution retraining should be individualized. The teacher should help the student diagnose the specific reasons for low performance on exams, while reminding the student of better performance on other tasks. Then suggest strategies for improvement and offer optimism. This might include help with test anxiety. Better preparation and over-learning can increase confidence and thus reduce anxiety. Relaxation techniques help. Extended time is a good idea for the student who's worried about time constraints. Sometimes it's the test atmosphere. I teach a class that meets in a large auditorium, and the tension on test day is "so thick you could cut it with a knife." I often let highly anxious students take the test somewhere else to avoid the group hysteria. After performing well on a test or two in a more comfortable environment, their self-confidence usually returns and they can then take the test with everyone else. Teachers can suggest such strategies, telling the student how they have helped other students to be successful.

Another important way in which students differ is *their parents*. Families are very different and obviously have a great impact on children's development. In order to give effective feedback and retrain attributions, teachers need to know about students' families. Chapter 4 discusses how to involve parents in your efforts to achieve gender equity.

STRATEGY 11: USE GROUPS EFFECTIVELY

Children tend to play in sex-segregated groups and have mostly same-sex friends. This exclusiveness often perpetuates sex-role stereotyping. Because one way to reduce reliance on stereotypes is to provide more information about the stereotyped group, it follows that having girls and boys learn more about each other will reduce stereotypes. Teachers often segregate girls and boys, which suggests to students that there must be very important educational differences between the two groups. *Teachers should make efforts to integrate classroom activities as much as possible.* Avoid having boys and girls line up separately or do different activities or compete against each other. Focus on "girls and boys together" and helping each other. Research has shown that in classes in which boys and girls work together, they hold less stereotyped views of each other.[15]

When teachers integrate groups, they usually sort the groups out to be half boys and half girls. This may perpetuate the idea that there's a battle between the sexes, and it's important to have a balance of power. Try experimenting with different compositions. Because boys tend to dominate girls, a group with half boys is likely to be male-dominated. If girls work either in all-girl groups or in equally mixed groups, they may learn that if boys are around, they will dominate. If groups are sometimes predominantly girls, then girls will have the opportunity to be leaders and to see girls in leadership roles with boys as followers. Boys, too, will have the experience of seeing girls in control of the group. Of course, having disproportionate groups means some groups will be predominantly male, but that too can be valuable experience because many adult women will find themselves situated in predominantly male work groups. You may need to monitor such groups to be sure that girls have a chance to contribute, or you may want to be sure that groups with a minority of girls have unusually assertive girls. Monitoring disproportionate groups can be difficult. Sometimes in groups with only a few boys, for example, girls end up "interviewing" the boys,[16] treating them almost as celebrities. The best advice is to be flexible with your groupings, change groups often, and give students the chance to work together in a variety of different groups with differing compositions. In all cases, you must monitor groups to be sure that everyone is contributing, no one is unfairly dominating the group, and that interpersonal problems are resolved.

Both boys and girls can benefit from working with a girl leader. Girl leaders will be accepted because of the legitimacy of their role, when they are appointed by a teacher, or because of their expertise. Teachers can provide girls with extra knowledge so that they are more likely to emerge as an informal leader. For example, if a new lesson will involve using a microscope, the teacher could instruct a small group of students, perhaps four or five girls and one boy, on how to use the microscope and then ask them to help others. Teachers can publicly acknowledge a girl's special expertise when it relates to a lesson, increasing the likelihood that she will emerge as an informal leader.

Another avenue for accepting a leader is through coercion or power: people will do what a leader says if the leader holds power over them. Unfortunately this basis for leadership has very negative consequences. Especially unfortunate is that this is just the kind of leadership power that teachers often assign girls. When teachers leave the room, for example, they are more likely to ask girls to take down names of people who misbehave. This type of power contributes to the negative stereotype of the girl who is a goody-two shoes and tattles to the teacher. Think of "Margaret" in the *Dennis the Menace* cartoon. She's no fun and it's no wonder that the boys don't want to play with her. *Encourage girls to be leaders based on their expertise.*

Cooperative learning is particularly effective at encouraging cross-group friendships and respect. Robert Slavin reports that cooperative learning leads to improved ability to see other people's perspective and results in better relations between different ethnic groups, increased self-esteem, and more tolerance of others.[17] Mixed sex groups may require a little more monitoring because girls and boys are not used to working together. Because boys tend to dominate groups, *teachers should assign clear roles.* Girls are more likely to assume a leadership role if it has been officially assigned and the boys acknowledge her right to be leader. Boys are less likely to dominate if a teacher or other adult is nearby. *Be sure your presence is felt* so that girls will feel freer to make contributions and boys will be inhibited from taking over. Observe the group's interactions and comment on any sex-typed behavior. Discuss with them why boys are talking more or why girls are being asked to write down ideas while boys generate them.

Cooperative learning requires expertise and commitment on the part of the teacher. When small, unstructured groups are used without significant teacher monitoring, sex-role stereotypes may even increase, because students are likely to act in stereotypical ways—boys assuming leadership, while girls assume a more passive role. Some studies show that girls achieve less when they are in mixed groups than when in all-girl groups.[18] You'll want to learn about the various strategies for implementing cooperative learning. The jigsaw method[19] is one such strategy, which may work especially well for gender equity. In this method, all groups study the same material. Each team member, however, is given a particular part of the lesson to learn and present to the others. Then the original groups split up, and new groups are formed, consisting of the students who are working on the same part of the lesson. These same-part groups help each other learn the material and also figure out the best way to present it. Students return to their original groups and each "expert" teaches his or her part of the lesson to the rest of the team. This method not only requires that girls take the role of teacher in their original groups, but it also includes figuring out how to teach the material as part of the learning process. Because being a teacher is usually considered a female task, it's not difficult for girls to assume a leadership role in the same-lesson groups. Boys are more willing to listen to girls' ideas about how to teach something than to their ideas in other domains. Thus the jigsaw method gives girls a legitimate leadership role, where making contributions doesn't require them to act in ways that might be interpreted as gender-inappropriate.

STRATEGY 12: TEACH THE "EVADED CURRICULUM"

The term, *evaded curriculum,* refers to what is not taught. Many topics that are central to the lives of girls and women are not included in the school curriculum. In the typical classroom, most of the curriculum revolves around Anglo-American men. It's not surprising that American history books, for example, focus on Anglo-American men because they have been in charge of our society. History lessons need to tell students who the leaders were and what they did. But teachers can *find interesting materials on the role of women and people of color, too.* This doesn't need to be restricted to lessons about individuals who had public accomplishments or activities. History can include "regular" people. A history lesson, for example, could include information about families during pioneer days.

Beware of books that include women or minority people as oddities. A book that only discusses them in separate boxes or in a separate chapter gives the impression that their contributions are only interesting asides. *Look for materials that integrate the contributions of women and people of color into the rest of the content.* Gretchen Wilbur suggests the following criteria for gender-fair materials:[20]

- They must acknowledge and affirm *variation*—that is, that women are not all the same.

- They must be *inclusive*—that is, they need to be about both women and men, as well as about people from different ethnic groups.

- They must be *accurate.*

- They must be *affirmative*—that is, they must stress the dignity and worth of all people.

- They must be *representative*—that is, they must present a balanced perspective.

- They must be *integrated*—that is, they must weave together the experiences and the lives of both women and men.

One often cited reason for the preponderance of male-oriented materials is that girls are willing to read about boys, but boys are reluctant to read about girls. It is possible that too many girl-related stories or materials might turn some boys off. Teachers should consider letting children choose materials, so that children will have the option of learning more about their own group. Trips to the library are an excellent way to both teach about the library, but also to allow students to select materials that are relevant to their own interests.

Materials about women are not the only topics that are evaded in the classroom. In general, little attention is given to feelings, interpersonal relationships, and emotional and sexual development. Career counseling needs to be more than information about jobs; it needs to include discussion of how both women and men can combine family and career. *Young girls need to learn about the topics that will help them deal with the issues that they will face as women in the twenty-first century.*

Most school librarians have information about appropriate resources. Teacher magazines are another source. Women's Educational Equity Act Program in Washington, D.C., has a number of interesting publications, such as Marlaine Lockheed's *Curriculum and Research for Equity: A Training Manual for Promoting Sex Equity in the Classroom* (WEEA Publishing Center, 55 Chapel Street, Newton, MA 02160). Ask, too, for their annotated bibliography of nonsexist resources. Women Educators publishes *Resource Directory for Sex Equity in Education* (care of Melissa Keyes, 300 N. Pinckney; Madison, WI 53703). The National Association for the Education of Young Children has published *Anti-Bias Curriculum: Tools for Empowering Young Children* (NAEYC, 1834 Connecticut Ave., NW, Washington, D.C. 20009-5786). Susan Klein's *Handbook for Achieving Sex Equity through Education* (1985, Baltimore: The Johns Hopkins University Press) is an excellent resource on all aspects of gender equity. Myra and David Sadker (1994), *Failing at Fairness: How America's Schools Cheat Girls* (New York: Scribners) includes an excellent list of resources. For specific examples of nonsexist activities see June Shapiro's *Equal Their Chances* (1982, Englewood Cliffs, NJ: Prentice Hall). Anne O'Brien Carelli's *Sex Equity in Education: Readings and Strategies* (1988, Springfield, IL: Charles C. Thomas) is an excellent resource (see especially, Dolores Grayson and Mary Martin's article on GESA [Gender Expectations and Student Achievement] training.) The Southern Poverty Law Center's *Teaching Tolerance* magazine is available free to teachers (400 Washington Ave., Montgomery, AL 36104). New materials are coming out all the time. Teachers should check ERIC indexes for the newest information.

Simply including more about women in the classroom won't equalize opportunity. But it will demonstrate that educators see girls and women as important and that their contributions to literature, art, science, math, history, and society are highly valued.

STRATEGY 13: FOCUS ON MATH AND SCIENCE

Math and science are the areas in which girls show their lowest performance levels as well as the lowest interest. While gender differences in math have been decreasing, differences in science achievement, however, are not decreasing; some evidence even suggests that they are *increasing*. The National Assessment of Educational Progress found that for nine-year-olds and thirteen-year-olds, gender differences in science achievement increased between 1978 and 1986.[21] Fewer young women take advanced math and science courses, but even when they do, they do not set the same career goals as their male counterparts. One study of high school seniors found that 64 percent of the young men who'd taken physics and calculus planned to go on and major in science or engineering. Only 18.6 percent of the young women taking those courses planned to major in science or engineering.[22]

Math and science is also, and not unrelatedly, the area in which negative stereotyping of women is most obvious. Math and science are a "critical filter," through which girls must pass in order to have access to many of the most prestigious and highest-paying careers.[23] An all-out effort is needed to involve girls more in math and science courses.

Although women's participation in math and science has been increasing, women still lag behind, particularly in the "hard" sciences. Developing girls' interest in these areas must start early; junior high school and high school is too late. By that time, most girls have already labelled math and physical science as male fields and have turned their interests elsewhere. A child's initial interest in science and math often starts very early and is fueled by play. Boys' toys and boys' play tend to have more of a scientific orientation. Naima Browne and Carol Ross (1991), in a study of young children's play, asked preschool children to sort toys into those that boys would play with and those that girls would play with.[24] Girls' toys were dolls, doll houses, pens, paper, and drawing materials. Boys' toys were building and constructions sets, such as "Lego" pieces or toy bricks, trucks, and cars. In their observations, Browne and Ross found that even when both girls and boys played with Legos, the girls made houses and furniture, which were used as secondary pieces in social play, while boys made vehicles, guns, and machines, often with elaborate, moving parts. Boys' constructions were more complex than girls.' Teachers had tried to encourage girls, but may have made things worse: when girls connected a few Lego pieces together, teachers responded with a great deal of praise. This, as you now know, suggested to the girls that not much was expected from them when it comes to construction. The same teachers encouraged boys to improve their models, often presenting problems that required redesign work.

Rose Parkin argues that construction play enhances spatial ability and contributes to later mathematical and scientific skills.[25] She succeeded in encouraging more construction play among preschool girls, but found that their play differed in ways that may influence their later development. Girls, for example, often built abstract patterns and designs with no stated goal, while boys were more likely to construct working models that involved more planning and problem solving. Boys were more confident in their use of materials and persisted longer on their models, correcting and improving them.

One of the "culprits" here is the notion of "free play." The kinds of play that provide unusually rich and varied spatial experience (such as construction play) are generally available during free-play time, which leads to their use mostly by boys, because such activities tend to be socially sex-typed as "boys' activities." Browne and Ross observed than even when girls tried to join boys in construction activity, they were usually rejected. When rejected, girls typically "settled" for another activity (usually a typical girls' activity) with no complaints. Teachers, therefore, rarely intervened to be sure girls were included in the building activity. Browne and Ross report that because boys tend to be more dominant, they more often got to play their first choice activity, while girls often moved to their second or third choice rather than fight for possession of a prized toy or for entry into a closed playgroup. Not surprisingly, boys often kept girls away from those activities that would have provided them with richer spatial experiences.

The problem with what occurs during free play is not limited to building activities. Early classroom experiences are typically divided into two categories, structured, required activities, versus free-play activities. Selma Greenberg analyzed the required activities (e.g., circle time, show and tell, story time, cutting, pasting, drawing, sorting, and stringing beads) and concluded that they focus on skill areas in which boys typically lag behind girls: verbal, social, and fine motor skills.[26] Further, the required activities emphasize impulse control, another area in which boys lag behind girls. Thus, these early, required activities focus on boys' weak areas. Among those *optional* activities, however (e.g., running, jumping, throwing, construction), are activities that emphasize large motor skills and varied spatial experiences—exactly those areas in which girls lag behind boys. Optional activities are typically the most sex-typed, which results in girls choosing activities at which they already excel, such as social play, doll play, or drawing. Boys dominate the "boy" activities, making it difficult for girls to choose these activities even if they want to. The result is that, because boys are required to engage in social, verbal, fine motor skills and because they choose to engage in the large motor and more spatial activities, they receive a broader range of learning experiences than girls. To ensure girls receive an equivalent variety of learning experiences, their needs and deficiencies need to be addressed just as systematically as those of boys.

The American Association of University Women's report that was discussed in Chapter 1 describes the great efforts that have gone into improving reading skills in early grades. Because poor reading has been more of a problem with boys, curricular specialists have made sure that reading materials were of particular interest to boys. Much money and effort also has been put into remedial programs and national advertising campaigns focused on literacy with male role models (such as athletes) urging boys to read. Improved literacy became a national priority. Now the same effort needs to be made with math and science education, with special emphasis on girls. Just as many teachers work to create a "Whole Language" classroom, where reading and writing permeate all aspects of daily school life, they now need to *create a "Whole Math and Science" classroom* in which math and science are incorporated into many and varied activities. Just as it's important for students to see teachers and other adults reading, it's important to see teachers and other adults doing math and scientific experiments.

It's especially important for girls to see women doing math and science. Lucy Sells founded the Math/Science Network, a group of over 1,000 scientists, educators, and community people dedicated to promoting and modeling female participation in science.[27] Other organizations can serve a similar purpose. For example, I've participated in "Science by Mail," a program in which I am a penpal to junior high students who are involved in science projects. Julie Cahill and Uma Pandya report on the "Craft Design Technology Project" in England.[28] In this program, female teachers and women from the community repair objects and engage students in simple repairs of bicycles and other machines, emphasizing problem solving, use of tools, and "tinkering."

The more that girls are exposed to female role models, the more they will begin to value math and science. Because math and science have been so heavily sex-typed, many women and girls perceive these fields as low in personal value. Students won't work hard to excel in subjects that they feel will not be of value to them. In fact, when Elizabeth Stage and her colleagues reviewed research on sex differences in math involvement, they found that the perceived value of math and confidence in one's ability were the two most critical variables in determining who pursued math education.[29] Making math and science more prominent in the curriculum, showing that it is an appropriate activity for both sexes, and developing girls' skills are important in reaching gender equity. Let's explore some strategies for doing that.

Teachers need to *be alert to ways in which they can relate math and science to topics that are of special interest to girls.* One geometry teacher I know starts the semester with a discussion and slide presentation of quilt patterns. There are many similar ways in which girls can be "eased into" more scientific modes of play. For example, to encourage girls to build more complex construction models, a teacher could start with a girl's simple model, as in the example below.

Teacher: "That's a nice house."
  Girl: "Yeah, it's for the mommy and the daddy and the baby."
Teacher: "You know, they might need some more rooms with three people living there."

Girl: "I could build another room."

Teacher: "Yes, but you know, their neighborhood is pretty crowded. maybe you should build a two-story house." *(Teacher presents a problem to be solved.)*

Girl: "Okay." *(She elaborates on the house, solving the problems that she encounters along the way.)* "There, now baby can sleep upstairs."

Teacher: "Oh, that's much better. Now they will have room. Remember when Sondra brought pictures of her grandparents' motor home? Maybe you could make your house into a motor home so the family could travel around." *(Teacher presents another design problem.)*

Girl: "Yeah! Then they could go to Disney World! I'll need wheels. . . ."

Teachers can present design problems and encourage girls to experiment to solve them. Browne and Ross described how one teacher started with girls' drawings of animals, encouraging them to make movable paper puppets of the animals, and finally to making models out of a construction set. Kim Beat suggests encouraging girls to build models, which then become the basis of a story or to have girls draw a plan for a house before building it.[30] She reports on the success of teaching a few girls a special skill, such as the use of a new piece of equipment, then having the girls teach the boys how to use it. This legitimizes girls' technical expertise and gets boys accustomed to taking a back seat when it comes to machines and equipment. Another suggestion that she makes is to engage children in special design projects, such as a house or a playground that would be accessible for children in wheelchairs.

Math and science need to be repositioned as gender-neutral fields. More female role models, more female teachers, and more female-oriented materials will help. Books and materials about women in math and science should be readily available to students.[31] Be sure that your school library has some prominently displayed.

Students rarely know much about careers. Career counseling needs to link math and science courses with a wide range of interesting careers. *The "human side" of math and science careers needs to be stressed.* Physicians and engineers, for example, should be more than technicians; by emphasizing the "people" side of male-dominated careers, these careers will be made more appealing to girls. Consider an architect. Buildings and homes designed by men sometimes overlook aspects that are salient to many women. Ask students to think about how women might approach building a house differently from men, or how children might approach the task differently from adults. One example is the placement of the toilet paper roll in most bathrooms. It's often placed so that it's difficult, if not impossible, for small children to reach. Ask boys and girls to describe the ideal kitchen, family room, or yard. Do they have different perspectives? Do their perspectives differ from those of adults? Talk with students about how designs can be improved by taking multiple perspectives. The auto industry is asking engineers to consider the physical requirements of women. For example, auto manufacturers now are realizing that cars designed by men sometimes overlook features that appeal to women or incorporate features that fit male body types and do not fit many women. Seats that don't go forward far enough, shoulder straps on seatbelts that don't fit a woman's body—these all point to the need for engineers to be aware of many physical differences. Fields such as engineering are not just about machines; they are about people interacting with machines. Scientists who design computer systems, for example, must be aware of the needs of the users. In the business world, managers focus not just on tasks, but on the people who perform them. Rather than simply focusing on the tasks that are required in careers, talking more about the people skills involved will attract more girls. It will also be a more realistic depiction of these careers and will result in better designs.

All students enjoy realistic assignments. A more hands-on, applied approach to teaching is highly motivating to both girls and boys. Higher-level math in particular is often taught in the abstract. Teachers need to focus on ways in which math can be used in domains that already interest girls. Sometimes the course content makes this difficult, but creative teachers can find ways to make the classroom more like the "real world." Grading systems can be based on real life. Some teachers use a "checkbook" system for evaluation. Students make deposits when they turn in homework or take a test. They make withdrawals if they fail to turn in work. Their "balance" determines their grade. Teachers can even add a "service charge" for grading late papers.

The most important element of all is for teachers, especially female teachers, to *show enthusiasm and excitement about math and science* and to convey that enthusiasm to girls. Girls' attention needs to be directed toward math and science, and teachers have to encourage (and expect) girls to become involved. Sometimes this may mean moving the boys out of the girls' way. In laboratories and in computer labs, for example, boys often take over, leaving girls to observe. Teachers need to *be sure that girls have equal access to equipment.* One study, for example, found that 49 percent of eleventh grade boys and only 17 percent of the girls had used an electricity meter.[32] Teachers often assign boy and girl lab team partners, and then find that the girl watches the boy perform the experiments. If, in class, boys dominate the discussion, the teacher should call on students more rather than relying on volunteers. Some teachers have had success with special science or math clubs targeted at girls. Go back to your gender-bias audit to see if there are special things that you can change to allow girls more participation in math and science.

Differential teacher behavior for girls and boys poses a special problem in science and math classes, both because these fields are more sex-typed and because many female teachers are not as comfortable with these subjects. To make matters worse, differences in teacher behavior toward girls and boys is usually found to be more extreme among students with high ability.[33] Thus, high-ability girls are more apt to lack self-confidence, doubt their abilities, and to downplay their successes.

Teachers need to *diagnose and remove impediments*. Besides problems such as equal access to equipment and resources, teachers should consider "math anxiety." Sheila Tobias has popularized the notion of math anxiety, and recent studies suggest that this anxiety can contribute to girls' lesser involvement with math.[34] Less emphasis on timed tests,[35] less competition, opportunities to retake exams, to correct mistakes, partial credit, more practice, and cooperative learning; all these strategies can reduce math anxiety.

As with the other strategies that we've discussed, these work well for boys as well as for girls. In fact, it may be that interest in science may decrease among boys, too, as the media perpetuates the "math/science nerd" stereotype. It's not just the negative way in which scientists are stereotyped or inadequate methods and materials for teaching science, but other changes have affected interest in science. When I was a child, children (usually boys) took machines apart to see how they worked. They "tinkered" with motors, telephones, toasters, and radios. Now, when you open a machine, you're likely to see nothing but a microchip. Now small appliances are replaced rather than repaired. Few children are exposed to role models who fix things at all and even fewer have an opportunity to tinker themselves. As I was working on this chapter, I was having trouble replacing a fanbelt on the lawn mower. No problem, I thought, my son has two friends over who are about to leave for college to study engineering, one at MIT and one at Rice University. They will be able to help. Neither had had any experience with lawn mowers ("Gee, my parents just pay someone to do that."), and one remarked that he hadn't realized lawn mowers had fanbelts. These boys, although talented at math and science, had lacked the opportunity to develop mechanical skills. More hands-on experience would have helped them.

SUMMARY OF THE STRATEGIES

You've learned thirteen ways to improve the learning environment. See if you can now expand on your action plan to achieve gender equity in your classroom. There's a lot to be done, so set realistic goals as you fill in the following Exhibit.

EXHIBIT

ACTION PLAN TO ACHIEVE GENDER EQUITY IN MY CLASSROOM

Long-Term	Next Semester	Expected Outcomes
Changes and additions that I will make in materials.		
Changes that I will make in the way that the course is organized or graded.		
Ways in which I will encourage goal setting.		
New feedback and attribution strategies that I will try.		
Changes that I will make in the way in which I interact with students.		
Ways in which I will encourage self-assessment.		

(continued)

Long-Term	Next Semester	Expected Outcomes
Ways in which I will encourage risk-taking.		
Ways in which I will help students learn from mistakes.		
How I will avoid negative messages.		
Ways in which I will reduce stereotyping.		
Ways in which I can use groups more effectively.		
How I can focus more on math and science with girls.		
Ways in which I can encourage girls in math and science.		

As a summary, the thirteen strategies are listed below. Review the list and be sure you fully understand each. Refresh your memory from time to time by returning to this list. Are you using all these strategies on a regular basis?

1. Perform a gender-bias audit of a classroom.

2. Teach self-assessment.

    ■ Ask students to predict how they will do on a task or test.

    ■ Have students evaluate their own work.

    ■ Having clear grading guidelines helps students evaluate their own work.

    ■ Use peer review.

    ■ Teach students to reward themselves for a job well done.

    ■ Ask for predictions on many things.

    ■ Get students to make predictions based on larger sets of data.

    ■ Model self-assessment.

    ■ Reward self-assessment.

3. Encourage risk-taking and help students to set goals.

    ■ Focus on learning goals whenever you can.

    ■ Focus on what students have learned, rather than on what they haven't learned.

    ■ Find alternative ways to recognize and reward learning.

    ■ Mastery learning techniques are especially good for learning goals.

    ■ Reduce the costs of failure.

4. Teach students to take pride in success, but to learn from mistakes.

    ■ Find ways to provide success to all.

    ■ Provide failure opportunities for all students.

    ■ Remind students of their successes.

    ■ Stop ruminations.

    ■ Perform a post mortem after failure.

    ■ Redefine failure as an opportunity.

- Redefine failure as diagnostic.
- Redefine failure as an expected stage that precedes success.
- Provide feedback without evaluation.

5. Provide good feedback.

- Give process feedback.
- Give positive regard rather than social reinforcement.
- Teach students how to seek feedback and help.
- Be aware of your own expectations and how they influence feedback.

6. Avoid negative messages.

- Avoid "low-ability" messages.
- Avoid "low-self-worth" messages.
- Avoid victim messages.
- Avoid negative nonverbal messages.
- Be aware of how teacher expectations can result in negative messages.

7. Retrain attributions.

- Link effort and performance.
- Emphasize pervasive, permanent, and internal explanations for success.
- Emphasize specific and temporary explanations for failure.
- Focus on choices and control.
- Teach optimism.

8. Reduce stereotypical thinking.

- Question stereotypes by seeking more information about individuals.
- Challenge your own stereotypes.
- Challenge students' stereotypes.
- Fight the media.
- Model gender-neutral behavior.
- Avoid sexist language.

- Value things feminine.
- Don't tolerate harassment of girls.

9. Redirect selective attention.

   - Focus attention on math and science.
   - Direct attention to choices rather than to barriers.
   - Redirect girls' attention to task-related information and redirect boys' attention to human relationships.
   - Redirect attention back to girls' comments or work.
   - Redirect attention to women's contributions.

10. Remember individual differences.

    - Find out as much as possible about each student as an individual.
    - Know where your students are educationally and what they're ready to learn.
    - Finding out more about your students requires attention to their individual reactions.
    - One individual difference for which teachers need to be alert is *helplessness*.
    - When suggesting more effort, be especially careful to be sure that the student has the necessary skills.

11. Use groups effectively.

    - Make efforts to integrate classroom activities as much as possible.
    - Encourage girls to be leaders, based on their expertise.
    - Use cooperative learning.
    - Assign clear roles.
    - Be sure your presence is felt.

12. Teach the "evaded curriculum."

    - Find interesting materials on the role of women and people of color.
    - Look for materials that integrate the contributions of women and people of color with the rest of the content.

- Teach young girls about topics that will help them deal with the issues that they will face as women in the twenty-first century.

13. Focus on math and science.

   - Create a "Whole Math/Science" classroom.

   - Be alert to ways to relate math and science to things that are of special interest to girls.

   - Reposition math and science as gender-neutral fields.

   - Stress the "human side" of math and science careers.

   - Show enthusiasm and excitement about math and science.

   - Be sure that girls have equal access to equipment.

   - Diagnose and remove impediments to girls' participation and enthusiasm.

ENDNOTES

1. Teachers interested in peer review should see Nystrand, M. (1986), "Learning to Write by Talking about Writing: A Summary of Research on Intensive Peer Review in Expository Writing Instruction at the University of Wisconsin-Madison." In M. Nystrand (ed.), *The Structure of Written Communication*. Orlando, FL: Academic Press. Or Anson, C. (ed.) (1989), *Writing and Response: Theory, Practice, and Research*. Urbana, IL: National Council of Teachers of English.

2. For a discussion of children and chess, see Horgan, D. (1987), "Chess as a way to teach thinking," *Teaching Thinking and Problem Solving, 9,* pp. 4–9; Horgan, D. (1992), "Lessons from chess." *INQUIRY: Critical Thinking Across the Disciplines, 10,* pp. 5–8; and Horgan, D. (1990), "Competition, calibration, and motivation," *Teaching Thinking and Problem Solving, 12,* pp. 5–10.

3. Horgan, D. (1992). "Children and chess expertise: The role of calibration." *Psychological Research, 54,* pp. 44–50.

4. Sharon Haggerty (1991) suggests that one reason for girls' difficulty in science is that they focus on learning right answers rather than on understanding ("Gender and School Science: Achievement and Participation in Canada," *Alberta Journal of Educational Research, 3,* pp. 195–208). A focus on asking questions, then, might be especially useful for girls.

5. For a discussion of learned helplessness and how to overcome it, see M. Seligman (1991), *Learned Optimism* New York: Alfred A. Knopf.

6. Stipek, D. (1993). *Motivation to Learn: From Theory to Practice*. Boston, MA: Allyn and Bacon.

7. For an indepth discussion of gender differences and differential implications of help-seeking, see Tannen, D. (1990), *You Just Don't Understand: Women and Men in Conversation*. New York: William Morrow and Co.

8. This checklist is based on the Brophy–Good Dyadic Interaction System as discussed and adapted in J. J. Irvine's (1991) *Black Students and School Failure: Policies, Practices, and Prescriptions*. New York: Praeger.

9. For some good ideas along this line, see Clifford, M. (1993), "Students Need Challenge, Not Easy Success," in A. Woolfolk (ed.), *Readings and Cases in Educational Psychology*. Boston, MA: Allyn and Bacon.

10. Seligman, M. (1991). *Learned Optimism*. New York: Alfred A. Knopf.

11. Perry, R.P., and Penner, K.S. (1990). "Enhancing Academic Achievement in College Student through Attributional Retraining and Instruction." *Journal of Educational Psychology, 82*, pp. 262–271.

12. Cazden, C. and Mehan, H. (1989). "Principles from Sociology and Anthropology: Context, Code, Classroom, and Culture." In M. Reynolds (ed.), *Knowledge Base for the Beginning Teacher*, American Association of Colleges for Teacher Education.

13. Stipek, D. (1993). *Motivation to Learn: From Theory to Practice*. Boston, MA: Allyn and Bacon, pp. 273–274.

14. Stipek (1993), p. 283.

15. Lockheed, M.E. and Harris, A.M. (1982). "Classroom Interaction and Opportunities for Cross-Sex Peer Learning in Science." *Journal of Early Adolescence, 2*, pp. 135–143.

16. Woolfolk, A. (1993). *Educational Psychology*. Boston, MA: Allyn and Bacon, p. 377.

17. Slavin, R. (1990). *Cooperative Learning*. Englewood Cliffs, NJ: Prentice Hall.

18. *AAUW Report: How Schools Shortchange Girls*. Washington DC: American Association of University Women Educational Foundation. p. 73.

19. For more information on this technique, see Aronson, E., Stephan, C., Sikes, J., Blaney, N., and Snapp, P. (1978). *The Jigsaw Classroom*. Beverly Hills, CA: Sage.

20. *AAUW Report: How Schools Shortchange Girls*. p. 64.

21. *AAUW Report: How Schools Shortchange Girls*. p. 26.

22. Dick, T. and Rallis, S. (1991). "Factors and Influences on High School Students' Career Choices," *Journal of Research in Math Teaching, 22*, pp. 281–292.

23. See Ernest, J. (1976), *Mathematics and Sex.* Santa Barbara, CA: University of California, Department of Mathematics.

24. Browne, N. and Ross, C. (1991). " 'Girls' Stuff, Boys' Stuff': Young Children Talking and Playing." In N. Browne (ed.), *Science and Technology in the Early Years*, pp. 37–51. Buckingham, Great Britain: Open University Press.

25. Parkin, R. "Fair Play: Children's Mathematical Experiences in the Infant Classroom." In N. Browne (ed.), *Science and Technology in the Early Years*, pp. 52–66. Buckingham, Great Britain: Open University Press.

26. Greenberg, S. (1985). "Educational Equity in Early Education Environments." In S. Klein (ed.), *Handbook for Achieving Sex Equity through Education*, pp. 457–469. Baltimore, MD: The Johns Hopkins University Press.

27. Sells, L. (1975). *Sex, Ethnic, and Field Differences in Doctoral Outcomes.* Unpublished doctoral dissertation. University of California, Berkeley.

28. Reported in Greenberg, S. (1985).

29. Cahill, J. and Pandya, U. (1991). "Challenging Sexism—Cycling Yesterday and Today: An Account of a Cross-Curricular Project." In N. Browne (ed.), *Science and Technology in the Early Years*, pp. 91–100.

29. Stage, E., Kreinberg, N., Eccles, J., and Becker, J., et al. (1985). "Increasing the Participation and Achievement of Girls and Women in Mathematics, Science, and Engineering." In S. Klein (ed.), *Handbook for Achieving Sex Equity through Education*, pp. 237–268.

30. Beat, Kim. (1991). "Design it, Build it, Use it." In N. Browne (ed.), *Science and Technology in the Early Years*, pp. 77–90.

31. Susan Klein. (1985). *Handbook for Achieving Sex Equity through Education* (Baltimore: The Johns Hopkins University Press) and the AAUW's *How Schools Shortchange Girls* are particularly good resources.

32. Mullis, L. and Jenkins, L. (1988). *The Science Report Card*, report no. 17-S-01. Princeton, NJ: Educational Testing Service, pp. 30–33.

33. Stage, E., Kreinberg, N., Eccles, J., and Becker, J., et al. (1985).

34. Tobias, S. (1978). *Overcoming Math Anxiety.* New York: Norton.

35. Tobias, S. and Weissbrod, C. (1980). "Anxiety and Mathematics: An Update." *Harvard Educational Review, 50*, pp. 63–70.

36. It has been suggested that female test takers are at a disadvantage on timed tests; see Goldstein, G., Haldane, D., and Mitchell, C. (1990), "Sex Differences in Visual–Spatial Ability: The Role of Performance Factors," *Memory and Cognition, 18*, pp. 546–550.

4 Dealing with Parents

Often, parents unintentionally convey low expectations to girls. The teacher's job is to do everything possible to help *every* child achieve and that means encouraging high expectations, not just among students, but also among their parents. The issue of gender socialization is highly value-laden. You may feel strongly that society is unfair to women. Not all parents will agree. You may feel that all sex-role stereotyping is wrong. Parents may believe just as strongly in sharply different roles for men and women. I'd suggest *not* starting your actions in these areas with a diatribe on sexism. Lecturing parents on how to raise their children rarely produces good results. The heavy-handed approach is likely to backfire.

All parents want their children to succeed. You can work toward that goal without advocating anything controversial and without forcing your political beliefs on parents. The techniques discussed in this book are good for all students and are not based on any political or social agenda. Many parents become upset when schools focus special attention on certain groups of students. Parents of boys are not likely to be pleased if you announce that you plan to devote a lot of time and attention to girls. Parents of boys probably feel that boys need extra time and attention, too. Parents want their child to get his or her fair share of resources. I've been at parents' meetings for scholastic chess in which parents of boys almost came to blows with parents of girls over some programs that the national chess association was advocating to encourage girls' participation. Resources in schools are often "zero sum games," where more money or attention for one group means less for another group. Parents fear that anything special for one group will take something away from their child's group.

When you "sell" your goals for your class to parents, it's best to emphasize how these goals will benefit all students. If you want to talk about de-emphasizing sex-role stereotypes, be sure to do it in a way that stresses benefits for all students and in a way that shows respect for parental values. Parents and teachers can only work together successfully when they share goals. Be sure to state your goals in such a way that they are consistent with parental goals.

Many parents are turned off by too much emphasis on social and emotional agendas. They want schools to focus on academics. If you want to talk about the dangers of sex-role stereotyping, be sure to tie your talk in with achievement. Consider the parents' perspective. I've fumed more than once at a fall orientation when a teacher has spent the entire session describing how she or he will build self-esteem and how the classroom management system works without once mentioning what the students will be reading or learning. Parents respect teachers' knowledge and expertise in teaching and in their subject matter. A good way to establish credibility, therefore, is by linking your goals to teaching and learning.

Based on what you've learned from this book, there are a few straightforward steps to dealing with parents. First, *listen* to parents. How do they explain their child's successes and failures? What expectations do they have for their child? Next, *share* with the parents. They may not be aware of their child's attributional style. Talk with them about how their child talks about success and failure. Does she downplay her success? Does she see her success as a fluke?

Listen to themes in the parent's attributions of their child's success or failure. Many parents see "only the best" in their child. They believe their child's failures are *your* fault; his or her successes are entirely due to their child's efforts and abilities. They may not give you any credit for their child's progress. If their child misbehaves, it's never his or her fault—it's the *other students'*. Other students' successes may be because you gave them extra advantages. As difficult as it is to work with these parents, the other extreme attribution style is much worse. This is when the parent sees "only the worst" in the child. If the child succeeds, it's a fluke, somebody must have helped, or the child cheated. Failure is expected and results from the child's low ability and low effort. In either case, the parents *interpret* what you say in light of their attributional style. Just as with students, your best bet is to retrain the attributions. To do that, you first have to figure out the pattern. Just as with the child, you can ask them what they think contributes to their child's successful and unsuccessful performance. Then listen for attributions that are *internal* such as *effort* or *ability* and those that are *external* such as *luck, task difficulty,* or *other people*.

Your guidelines for giving feedback to parents are just like those for students:

- Link effort and performance
- Emphasize pervasive, permanent, and internal explanations for success

- Emphasize specific and temporary explanations for failure

- Focus on choices and control

- Be optimistic

Let's consider a hypothetical conference between "Ms. Ramirez," a fourth-grade teacher and "Mr. and Mrs. Jones," parents of "Janet," who is having problems in math. Ms. Ramirez has called the meeting after sending home report cards. She's pleased that both parents responded immediately. She has not met either parent, but suspects from their address that they are not affluent. Ms. Ramirez is well prepared. She has put together a folder of Janet's work in math as well as in other subjects. Ms. Ramirez is confident, because she's a veteran teacher and knows how to handle parents. She greets Mr. and Mrs. Jones warmly at the door and shows them around the room, pointing out Janet's seat and explains the organization of the classroom, the student work displayed, and the themes for social studies during this six weeks. She's careful to avoid educational jargon and is warm and friendly, even introducing herself by her first name. She wants Janet's parents to feel welcome and comfortable and a part of Janet's educational process. She seats them in the front of the room in chairs from the teachers' lounge so that they will not have to sit in "little" chairs. She's careful not to intimidate them by sitting behind her rather imposing desk, but sits adjacent to them in the same kind of chair as they have. She asks them for questions and comments and listens carefully to them so as not to monopolize the discussion. She maintains eye contact, is unhurried, and lets them know that she considers their daughter to be very important. Mr. and Mrs. Jones seem relaxed and comfortable. Ms. Ramirez is pleased with how well this is going.

Ms. Ramirez: I'm so glad you've come in today. Janet is such a beautiful little girl. I know how proud you must be of her. (Smiling to herself, Ms. Ramirez thinks, "I'm *starting on a positive note,* just like I learned in my teacher education program.")

(Note: While this is a nice thing to say about Janet, Ms. Ramirez is basing her compliment on Janet's appearance (an external attribution). Janet has little control over her appearance. It would be much better for Ms. Ramirez to compliment Janet on something internal such as ability or effort (e.g., "Janet works so hard and is such a bright little girl") Would Ms. Ramirez have complemented the physical appearance of a boy? Further, Ms. Ramirez has implied that Janet's parents ought to base their evaluation of Janet on her appearance.)

Ms. Jones: Yes, Janet has never given us any trouble. She's always been a little lady.

(Note: This comment suggests her parents may hold stereotypical notions about sex roles.)

Ms. Ramirez: I enjoy having her in my class. And she's doing very well. She's a good little helper and always helps me clean up. I can tell she's been well trained at home!

(Note: This comment, too, is nice, but focuses on Janet's social behavior. Ms. Ramirez may be sending the message that being a good helper is more important than being a good student. We're well into the discussion and schoolwork hasn't even come up. If Janet were a boy, would Ms. Ramirez be putting so much emphasis on appearance and helpfulness?)

Ms. Ramirez: I've got some of Janet's work here, and I thought we could all look at it. As you can see, she's done very well in reading and social studies. She likes those subjects. The problem is in math. You'll notice that she's missing some homework assignments and others are incomplete.

Mrs. Jones: Well, I guess I'm not surprised. I was never any good in math either. Luckily I never have to use algebra!

Ms. Ramirez (laughing): I know what you mean. We girls aren't much for math, are we? (Ms. Ramirez is proud of how she's empathizing with the parents and making them feel comfortable.)

(Note: This would have been an ideal time for a little "attribution talk." Ms. Ramirez has allowed inferences to be made that (1) girls aren't good in math, (2) girls don't like math, (3) it's okay for girls not to do well in math, and (4) that math skill is unrelated to effort. She should have put an emphasis on the evidence that effort was lacking. She also should have made some statement about the value of math for girls and debunked the idea that girls aren't good in math.)

Mr. Jones: What do you think is Janet's problem?

Ms. Ramirez: Well, lots of girls have trouble with math. Janet is a good reader, but she needs to make better grades in math. She has to pass math to go on to the fifth grade, you know. I can help her after school. And maybe, Mr. Jones, you can help her with her homework? Math is hard and Janet will need help. (Ms. Ramirez is again pleased with herself because she's offered a constructive plan and has been careful not to be too critical of Janet.)

(Note: Ms. Ramirez explained Janet's success in reading by reference to a general trait: she's a "good reader." Her explanation for her failure in math revolves around her "needing help." This suggests that Janet lacks the ability. Ms. Ramirez also suggests that

a father would be more help than a mother. [This might be true in some families, particularly in later grades, but Ms. Ramirez should have not assumed the father was good in math without any evidence.] The emphasis is on others' helping Janet, rather than on Janet putting more effort in. Ms. Ramirez also needs to be more specific about the skills Janet needs to develop. Janet's failure in math seems like a general and pervasive problem. The only reason Ms. Ramirez has given for Janet to improve is so that she can pass. Ms. Ramirez has not made the goal of doing well in math seem very important nor tied it to other important goals.)

Mr. Jones: Well, I think I can help her. We'll set aside some time every night. What in particular should we work on?

Ms. Ramirez: Oh, I think you should go over her homework and be sure she's comfortable with what we're doing. I'll meet with her on Tuesday afternoons and help her catch up.

(Note: Mr. Jones seemed to be ready to focus on something specific, but Ms. Ramirez resisted. She continued to make this sound like a general and pervasive problem. She should have been prepared with an analysis of Janet's work and standardized test scores to show that the problem is not a general lack of ability, but more specific. Perhaps Janet does well on calculations, but has trouble with word problems. Perhaps there were one or two units that gave her more difficulty. When dealing with an academic problem, it's important to emphasize specific and temporary explanations for failure. It's also important to send the message that improvement is under the student's control. So far Ms. Ramirez has not emphasized that theme.)

In this example, the parents were easy to deal with, non-defensive, and eager to help. But we see that Ms. Ramirez failed to link effort and performance. She perpetuated the stereotype that girls aren't expected to do well in math. Janet may do better in math as a result of more help, but she's unlikely to change her attitudes toward math or be anxious to choose challenging math courses later.

Now, let's consider a "problem" parent. "Mr. LaRue" teaches 7th grade English and has scheduled a conference with "Dewayne's" mother. Dewayne is a major behavior problem in class and is failing the course. Like Ms. Ramirez, Mr. LaRue has prepared carefully for this meeting and is careful to establish rapport with "Ms. Moore," Dewayne's mother.

Mr. LaRue: I guess you know I'm having some problems with Dewayne.

Ms. Moore: I don't know why. Dewayne never gives me any problems. Some teachers just don't know how to handle boys his age. He's doing fine in his other classes.

(Note: Ms. Moore is attributing Dewayne's problems to external factors—the teacher.)

Mr. LaRue: It is difficult to handle boys of this age. But let's look at what's happened this semester. I have my records here. Dewayne has received five marks for talking in class; he's been sent to the principal for fighting in class; he's been tardy ten times. That kind of behavior makes it difficult for me to conduct my class.

(Note: Mr. LaRue has appropriately focused on specifics and how Dewayne's behavior has affected him.)

Ms. Moore: Well, I know about that fight and the other boy started it. He's tardy sometimes because his 3rd period teacher goes past the bell. As for talking, he does that because he's bored.

This is a classic case of a parent blaming external factors for her child's failures. At this point, Mr. LaRue knows he has a long and difficult retraining job ahead. He will need to consistently, throughout the year, at every opportunity, with both Ms. Moore and Dewayne, stress Dewayne's own lack of effort as a major contributor to his poor performance. He must also interpret Dewayne's failures in terms of specific behaviors and offer specific suggestions for improvement that are under Dewayne's control. Now that Mr. LaRue has heard Ms. Moore's attributional style, he's not surprised that Dewayne has learned to explain his failure by blaming others.

Mr. LaRue will need to think of ways to get this message across. He may want to set some very specific rules for Dewayne's performance; perhaps a contract that if he receives no marks for disturbances in class and no tardiness, he will earn a plus for his conduct grade. Mr. LaRue will need to be very certain that his classroom management techniques demonstrate a clear and consistent linking between Dewayne's behavior and the outcomes. When Mr. LaRue talks about behavior in class (whether it's Dewayne's or someone else's), he needs to use appropriate attributional explanations. When Dewayne or his mother offer external explanations for Dewayne's problems, he will need to offer disconfirming evidence. This will need to be done tactfully. Mr. LaRue knows other teachers are having similar problems with Dewayne. They need to talk together and all work to send the same attributional messages.

Ms. Moore is typical of many parents. Parent training programs need to focus on explanations of success and failure. Mr. LaRue would be wise to suggest a PTA workshop dealing with these issues. As exasperating as it is to deal with Ms. Moore, the parent who consistently blames the child for everything that goes wrong is worse. At least Ms. Moore is giving her child support. Think about it: if parents were completely objective about their own children, parenting would be even more difficult! Believing the best about a child is better than believing the worst. Imagine if every time a child did something wrong, the parent responded,

"Well, of course. You're stupid and lazy." (A general and pervasive internal attribution.) That's the pattern shown in the following example.

"Mr. Biggs" teaches 11th grade Spanish. "Cynthia" is doing poorly and Mr. Biggs has, after several attempts, finally arranged for her father to come to school. Mr. Biggs knows from his prior experience that "Mr. Epstein" will be difficult, and so he's prepared carefully and is ready to be at his most charming.

> *Mr. Biggs:* I'm glad you were able to make it. I wanted to talk about Cynthia's Spanish grade before it got any worse. There's still time for her to bring it up if we can just get her motivated.
>
> *Mr. Epstein:* Trying to motivate Cynthia is a waste of time. She's lazy. Always been that way and always will. Frankly I just don't expect much from her. She's never done well in school. Some kids have it and some don't. I'll be happy if she just stays out of trouble.
>
> *Mr. Biggs:* I think Cynthia can do well. Look at her test scores: they're above average, so I know she's capable. Look at her grades so far. They're all low except for the test on culture. She made a B! That's because she found that part interesting and she did her homework. See, that row of numbers represents homework. It's mostly empty except for Unit 4, on Spanish culture. I talked with her history teacher—she's doing well in that class. It looks to me as if she can do well when she's interested and puts forth more effort. What we need to do is to get her interested in her other courses. I think Cynthia could be a good student if she puts her mind to it.

(Note: Mr. Biggs linked effort and performance, gave evidence of general ability, pointed to specific and temporary explanations for her failure, stressed Cynthia's control over her performance, and was optimistic. Hopefully, he's also realistic about retraining Mr. Epstein. This one conversation won't do it. He must send these same messages to Mr. Epstein and Cynthia many times. He must also build up Cynthia's self-esteem and confidence. This is a student who will need lots of positive regard. She will need to be reminded of her successes and her role in those successes repeatedly.)

Cynthia is a student who is at risk for serious problems. Mr. Biggs may want to discuss her problems with the guidance counselor or school psychologist. Unfortunately, there are many parents such as Mr. Epstein. While Ms. Moore and Mr. Epstein represent mirror-image problems, notice that the same attributional rules apply across the board:

- Link effort and performance

- Emphasize pervasive, permanent, and internal explanations for success

- Emphasize specific and temporary explanations for failure

- Focus on choices and control

- Be optimistic

Teachers can teach these lessons through modeling, through reference to characters in literature or history, and through explanations of classroom behavior. Obviously the extent to which each suggestion is stressed depends on the particular attributional style of the student or parent.

Although students often learn how to explain their success or failure from their parents, sometimes students and parents have different attributional styles. Parents who are eager to blame their children for failures and not give them credit for their successes may force a child into a defensive stance. If nothing the child does results in a favorable response from parents, the child will understandably come to blame failure on external causes, "Everyone's against me, nothing's fair." The child has learned to blame others to maintain some self-respect. Here, too, teachers can help by sending consistent attribution messages. The child's response, although a problem for the teacher, is healthier than learned helplessness. Some children come to believe they are helpless (and worthless) from the messages that their parents send.

When dealing with parents, it's essential to remember that parents, teacher, and students may have very different interpretations of school performance. These are difficult to change, but sending consistent appropriate attributional messages and disconfirming inappropriate messages is the best approach. The disconfirming evidence should be objective and diplomatically presented.

Teachers often misunderstand and misinterpret parents' behavior. Negative beliefs about different ethnic groups or about lower socioeconomic parents can set the stage for an ineffective meeting.[1] Remember that stereotyping is something all humans do! Sometimes teachers become adept at pointing out gender or racial stereotypes in children's books and in the media and overlook their own stereotypes. Before a conference, stop and think what you expect from different parents. Are you making assumptions based on the child's performance? On the child's style of dress? On where the child lives? On the parent's occupation? In the exercise below, jot down your expectations. Which parents do you suspect will be defensive? Which will question your competency? Which will deny there's a problem? Which will you feel comfortable or uncomfortable with? Who might be intimidated by you? Who might intimidate you? If you were then meeting with that parent, you would want to focus on evidence to disconfirm your expectation.

EXHIBIT

Situation

Expectation

Brittany's parents are very wealthy
and went to Ivy League schools.

Sam comes to school in rumpled
clothes, often wearing the same
thing several days in a row.

Eduardo comes from a large family
of Mexican descent. He speaks with
a strong accent.

Drew's father is an attorney, and
Drew has threatened that "if you
give me a hard time, my dad will
sue you."

Anne's mother is a prominent local
businesswoman. Anne's not doing
well in school and has been
very upset because, in her words,
"My mom will kill me if I don't
make all A's."

Situation	Expectation
You heard a rumor that Kirsten's mother complained to the school board last year when Kirsten didn't make cheerleader.	_____ _____ _____ _____
Matthew's father is the minister at a local conservative church.	_____ _____ _____ _____

A useful lesson in the limitations of stereotypes is to visit a school function in junior high or high school and see if you can match the students with their parents. I'll bet you see well dressed parents with scruffy children, scruffy parents with well dressed children, overweight parents with skinny children, skinny parents with overweight children, polite parents with obnoxious children, obnoxious parents with polite children, shy parents with outgoing children, outgoing parents with shy children, and so forth.

One of the delights of working with people is the continual surprise. Look for "surprises" when you meet with parents, rather than waiting for them to confirm your expectations. If you find your expectations and stereotypes taking over, remind yourself of some of your bigger surprises.

One of a teacher's most important jobs is to involve parents in their child's education. You'll want to provide parents with information as well as support. Establish a lending library of resources. Consider an orientation meeting for parents, a newsletter, handouts and other ways of letting them know what you expect from their students and the kinds of activities they will be doing in your class. Be sure to communicate clearly and without condescension or jargon. Be positive. State rules in terms of what you want the students to do, rather in terms of "do nots." Telephone chains are another way to involve parents. Find upbeat ways to communicate. Don't limit communications to problems; call or send notes to praise students. Encourage parents to call you or send notes to school. Just as you want to be sure each child has more success than failure, be sure each parent receives more good news than bad news about their child. Remember that if there is a problem, it's much better if you and the parent already have established a working relationship and trust.

Parents will usually come to school to see their child perform. Invite parents for classroom plays, shows, and exhibits. Even oral book reports or poetry recitations can become an event. Be sure there are many opportunities, scheduled at convenient times, when parents can be involved in your classroom. Involve parents in projects that have a high likelihood of success. If parents volunteer and see positive effects of their efforts, they will be eager to continue helping. Find enthusiastic parents to help you bring in other parents. Involve students in efforts to bring in parents. Students can design invitations or publish a class newspaper. The more involved the parents are, the more successful you will be at reducing gender bias.

ENDNOTES

1. For some good suggestions, see Irvine, J.J. (1991). *Black Students and School Failure: Policies, Practices, and Prescriptions.* New York: Praeger; Hernandez, Hilda (1989). *Multicultural Education: A Teacher's Guide to Content and Process.* New York: Merrill; and Banks, J. A. and McGee C. A. (1993). *Multicultural Education: Issues and Perspectives,* Second Edition. Needham Heights: Allyn and Bacon.

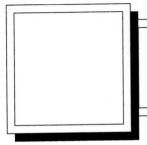

Epilogue

EVALUATING THE RESULTS AND KEEPING UP THE GOOD WORK

In order for you to maintain your energy and enthusiasm for reducing gender bias, you need to see results. Sometimes day-to-day results are so gradual that you are unaware of them. Make notes about students' progress throughout the year. Have students write success and failure stories at the beginning of the year and again at the end. Review how they change over the year. Keep track of students' predictions. Does accuracy increase over the year? As the year progresses, do students bring in more examples of sex-role stereotypes from the media? Do you hear students disconfirming each others' inappropriate attributions? Go back to some of the worksheets in Chapter 3. Would the answers be the same now?

Many teachers ask students to write essays at the beginning of the year. Suggest that students write about their expectations, career goals, or plans for high school. Ask them to write on the same topic at the end of the year. See if girls have raised their expectations and broadened their goals. Look for success from your efforts to motivate yourself to continue.

You need to remind yourself to keep up with the program. Keep the following checklist handy and, every week or so, go through and be sure you're doing everything you can to maximize your students' success.

WEEKLY CHECKLIST

☐ Have I made sure that each student experienced more success than failure?

☐ Have I linked effort and performance?

☐ When a student worked hard and wasn't successful, have I developed a strategy so that he or she can be successful in the future?

☐ Have I focused on learning rather than performance goals?

☐ Have I helped my students analyze successful and unsuccessful events?
    ☐ Have I offered optimistic analyses?
    ☐ Have I helped them put success or failure in a larger context?
    ☐ Have I helped students redefine failure as an opportunity for growth?
    ☐ Have I made sure students learned from their mistakes?

☐ Have I given extra feedback? Especially process feedback and disconfirming feedback?

☐ Have I encouraged students to seek feedback on their own?

☐ Have I avoided negative messages?

☐ Has my praise been sincere and truthful? Have I avoided excessive praise for mediocre performance?

☐ Have I formulated extra praise in terms of internal attributions after student success?

☐ Have I discussed progress towards goals and plans?

☐ Have I encouraged risk taking?

☐ Have I intervened when students focused exclusively on obstacles and barriers and emphasized choices and control?

☐ Have I been a good role model?
    ☐ Have I shared my problem-solving strategies?
    ☐ Have I talked appropriately about my successes and failures?
    ☐ Have I modeled gender-neutral activities?

☐ Have I incorporated examples of successful women and minorities into my lessons?

☐ Have I debunked stereotypes?

☐ Have I discouraged harassment of girls?

☐ Have I made a special effort to encourage girls in math and science?

☐ Have I made an effort to use group work to motivate and encourage girls?

☐ Have I taken individual differences into account?

☐ Have I done something to involve parents?

At the end of the semester, go back to your Action Plan. Did you accomplish everything you'd planned? Did you achieve the expected outcomes? Re-assess both your plans and the results. If you weren't successful, do a post mortem. Set another group of subgoals for next semester. Gender bias in the school is a long-standing problem; changing will take a long time. At this point, you should be aware of the inequities and their negative effects. You should also be aware of how your own behavior and expectations can either add to or reduce bias. You now have to find which strategies work well for you in your particular classroom and practice them until they become your normal mode of interaction. Eliminating gender bias is a big project, but it's too important to postpone. The twenty-first century is just around the corner. I won't wish you luck on this project because your efforts and ability, rather than luck, will determine your success. Instead I'll say, "Happy efforts and much well deserved success."

Index